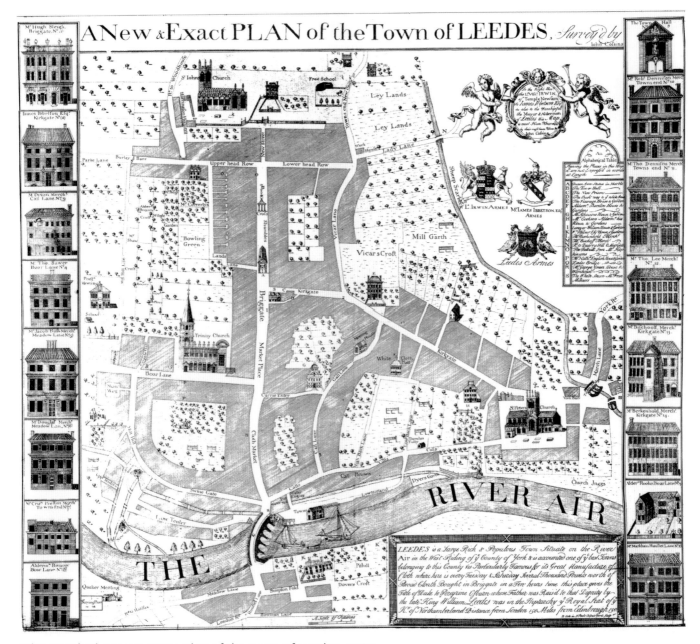

John Cossins', New & Exact Plan of the Town of Leedes, 1726.

Cover image: The South-East Prospect of Leeds, in the County of York, by Samuel and Nathaniel Buck. Published according to Act of Parliament April 15th 1745.

Published by Leeds City Council 2016
© Steven Burt and Kevin Grady.
© New artwork Peter Brears.

ISBN No. 978-1-5262-0543-8

A History of Kirkgate
from earliest times to 1800

by Steven Burt and Kevin Grady

Illustrations by Peter Brears

Preface

Kirkgate has existed for well over a thousand years and, with its church, it is the original settlement from which the great modern city of Leeds has sprung. When we wrote The *Illustrated History of Leeds* in 1994, we were unable to devote much space to the form of the original village. The creation of the Lower Kirkgate Townscape Heritage Initiative in 2012 to promote the regeneration of the historic heart of Leeds gave us the stimulus to intensively research and write a history of Kirkgate from its Anglo-Saxon, perhaps ancient British, origins to the present day. Such has been the extent of fascinating new material that we have unearthed that the small booklet we had intended has grown like Topsy. To do justice to the subject we decided for the present to limit ourselves to taking the story up to 1800 by which time the era of the great gentlemen merchants of Kirkgate was almost at an end.

We have had three principal purposes in writing the book. The first is to explain why the First White Cloth Hall is the most important historic building in Leeds city centre and why it must be regenerated as one of the jewels of the city's heritage. The second is to demonstrate clearly that Kirkgate, The Calls and the site of Leeds Minster are the site of the original settlement of Leeds and that all opportunities for their archaeological investigation must be taken. Thirdly, we want to share our fascinating new found knowledge with our fellow citizens.

Reconstructing the past is often a very complex task, especially when dealing with very fragmentary evidence. Some of the biggest but most rewarding challenges have been interpreting the evidence which has allowed us to reconstruct the form of the village of Leeds in 1089 and 'rebuild' the 15th century Hall of Pleas and bakehouse. Equally challenging but ultimately greatly pleasing, has been the work to establish the original form of the First White Cloth Hall, and to reconstruct the appearance of our hero Ralph Thoresby's Kirkgate house, garden and museum.

Periodically throughout the book there are topic pages with a pink background. These allow us to provide additional information about topics of special interest which otherwise would have interrupted the flow of the main narrative.

When reading this book it is helpful to bear in mind that in the Middle Ages the name Leeds, indeed 'Loidis', 'Leedis' or 'Leedes', was applied to several different things. There was the parish of Leeds which included not only the village based on Kirkgate but also the associated hamlets of Woodhouse and Knostrop and, with their villages, the manors of Hunslet, Holbeck, Beeston, Armley, Bramley, Wortley, Farnley, Headingley-cum-Burley, Potternewton and Chapel Allerton. Then there was the manor of Leeds which originally comprised Kirkgate and extensive lands stretching out to Woodhouse and Knostrop. Within the bounds of the manor of Leeds, from 1089 there was the manor of Leeds-Kirkgate and from 1207 the manorial 'borough of Leeds', the street we know today as Briggate.

We hope you enjoy the book. Read on!

Contents

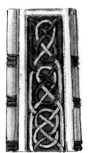

The Leeds Crosses. From the large number of carved stones found in the rubble of the parish church tower in 1838, Peter Brears has been able to visually reconstruct the original form of two of the Leeds crosses; these display a curious mixture of pagan and Christian images. On the left is the 13 feet tall, early tenth-century, 'Church Cross' which physically reconstructed stands today in Leeds Minster. Its front features in the lowermost panel Weland the Smith, a Danish mythical hero, in his flying machine. Above it is a robed figure holding a book, probably St Matthew, and above him the haloed figure in blue, with the eagle above, is very likely to be St John. The side of the cross has a vine scroll with leaves and fruit.

The smaller cross, on the right, also has Weland the Smith in its lowermost panel, and above it a figure, thought to be St John the Evangelist, holding a book and with a bird on his shoulder. Above is a figure holding a book in two hands, probably also an evangelist; uppermost is another evangelist holding a book.

These very expensive monuments were originally coated in plaster and brightly painted. On their right we see examples of the fine interlaced strap work found on the crosses. Above them is an intriguing stone bearing the runes CUNU[NG] ONLAF, translating as King Onlaf. Though found with the crosses in the rubble of the church tower, probably it was not part of one of them but was a fragment of a separate longer inscription relating to one of the Viking kings of York during the second quarter of the tenth century, either Anlaf Sihtricsson or Anlaf Guthfrithsson. The presence of a royal inscription of this kind is very rare, and appears to show that Leeds had some claims to importance at this time.

The Origins of Kirkgate

Leeds Parish Church – South Aspect in 1715.
(Ducatus Leodiensis)

A wonderful discovery

In 1838 workmen began to demolish the old parish church of St Peter in order to prepare the site for a splendid new building. Once the roof had been removed they began to knock down the walls. The most hazardous task was to demolish the tower; great care was taken as each stone was lowered to the ground. Just below the old bell-chamber a strange carved stone was discovered. Many additional pieces were found and it soon became apparent that some of them could be joined together. Soon a pillar of a massive stone cross 13 feet high had been assembled and there were pieces for another six crosses left over.[1] These remarkably elaborately carved Viking crosses had clearly been erected in the graveyard of a church on this site in the early tenth century when Leeds was part of the Viking kingdom of York. The stones featured both Christian and pagan scenes. They established beyond question that Leeds had been a place of importance in the early Middle Ages.

Leeds and its first church

'Leeds' is derived from the British word 'Loidis' which was first used to describe the people living by the river but later it was applied to a region of the British kingdom of Elmet and ultimately to a single important place within it. Leeds may even have been the last independent capital of Elmet before the British kingdom was overwhelmed by the advancing Anglo-Saxons early in the seventh century. It is located on a strategic river crossing where the narrow Aire valley, at the eastern edge of the Pennines, opens on to the broad lowlands of the Vale of York. The valley was a natural east-

west route-way across the Pennines which was much used in ancient times. A second route to Leeds crossed the mountain range from the south-west via Standedge where the Pennines are at their narrowest.[2] The convergence of the two routes made Leeds a natural site for settlement. It became an ideal meeting place for early settlers. The original settlement at Kirkgate was created in the area of well-drained land located between two ancient trackways that began at the ford across the River Aire just below Leeds Bridge. The first trackway, today known as The Calls, headed north-east towards York, the age old capital of the British kingdom of Deira (subsequently the Anglo-Saxon kingdom of Northumbria). It passed below the Iron Age hill fort on Quarry Hill dating to approximately 600 B.C. The second followed what is now Call Lane and Vicar Lane, heading north to the Wharfe valley and the ford across the river at Harewood.

The Anglo-Saxons had initially been pagan but Britain became a target for missionaries sent from Rome to convert the heathens to Christianity. In 625 A.D. one of these missionaries, Paulinus, became the chaplain of Princess Ethelburga of Kent. When she married King Edwin of Northumbria he too became a Christian and actively promoted his new faith. Around 730 A.D. the monk, the Venerable Bede, recorded in his 'Ecclesiastical History of the English Nation', that King Edwin, after conquering the kingdom of Elmet, set up there a royal house where Paulinus built a wooden church.[3] Some historians have suggested that this church may have been on the present site of the Leeds Minster. Perhaps we will never be certain but by the Anglo-Saxon period a large earthwork had been constructed on the site of the Minster across the trackway to York. Being near the confluence of the River Aire and Sheepscar beck and at the edge of the marshy ground, it provided a safe haven for settlers. The Anglo-Saxons appear to have used this as an early Christian missionary centre. Its isolated location near a major river crossing, a tributary and the edge of marshy ground mirrors that of the minster church at Dewsbury. Given the tenuous nature of the information available, such theories must be treated with caution.[4]

It was the next wave of invaders, the Vikings, who left the first compelling evidence that Leeds, based on Kirkgate, was an important early settlement. The Viking attacks began in 793 A.D. but it would be almost eighty years before they actually started to settle in the Leeds area. By the time of Alfred the Great (871-899 A.D.) much of the country was under Danish rule, including Leeds. When Christianity was being re-established in the seventh century, crosses were sometimes used to mark 'preaching centres' before a church could be built but by the time of the Leeds crosses, preaching crosses were unnecessary because churches were well established. This group of crosses confirms Leeds as an important ninth century settlement because they must have been memorials to lordly Viking settlers who thought Leeds of sufficient distinction to choose it as their place of burial.

Also found among the demolition rubble in 1838 were the remnants of one or more hogbacks, expensive Viking grave covers or memorial stones, to commemorate the burial place of an important local leader. The crosses are very likely to have been funerary monuments to them and other powerful Vikings in the area.[5] Significantly the name 'Kirkgate' is itself Old Norse meaning the 'road to the church'. The street was strategically located near the river ford and next to the large enclosed site of the manorial hall beside the churchyard, where a powerful Scandinavian family lived who would have been the main benefactors of the church.[6]

St Peter's was the ecclesiastical centre for a much larger area than the manor. The priest ministered to his parish, which comprised not only the inhabitants of the manor of Leeds but also those of the manors of Allerton, Gipton, Osmondthorpe, Beeston, Hunslet, Holbeck, Wortley, Bramley, Armley and Headingley; in all an area of around thirty-two square miles.

The manorial hall and church in 1089. (Peter Brears; hereafter all illustrations by Peter Brears are indicated by 'PB')

Norman Kirkgate

The Norman Invasion

The first firm documentary evidence about Leeds is found in the Domesday Book. When William the Conqueror invaded England in 1066 he brought with him a vast entourage of men who were keen to profit from the venture. England was the best administered country in Europe and had consequently become one of the wealthiest. William desperately needed taxes to pay his army and keep it fed. In 1086 he ordered a survey of all these conquered lands which became known as 'The Domesday Book'.[7] This provides the first detailed written record of the settlement of Leeds. His commissioners, interpreters and scribes arrived on horseback along the road from Thorpe Stapleton.[8] The villagers had already suffered at the hands of the victorious army, being press-ganged into helping to dig the ditches and construct the wooden palisade of the new fort to the west of the village, near the strategically important crossing point of the Aire.

The scribes noted that, before the conquest, Leeds had been divided between seven thegns, members of the highest echelon of Anglo-Scandinavian society who held their land from the king or one of his powerful retainers usually in return for military service.[9] The community now lacked these leaders, who were either dead or powerless to defend them from the might of the Norman army. William had given the manor to Ilbert de Lacy, a Norman baron, with enormous estates in France, Lincolnshire and the Midlands. He was also lord of the vast area of land known as the honour of Pontefract and leader of the powerful army that dominated the area and subjugated the local population.

Nevertheless there was still a hierarchy within the manor without the thegns: there were 4 sokemen (the free tenants), followed by 27 villeins (unfree tenants), and 4 bordars (cottagers). These men and their families constituted a population of around two hundred people who laboured in the open fields that extended from the main village on Kirkgate out to Knostrop to the east and Woodhouse to the north, 1320 acres of prime farmland. Fourteen plough teams were needed for the six ploughs required to till the ground. St Peter's church continued to minister to the needs of the parish and the scribes diligently recorded the presence of a priest and the fact that the village already had a corn mill on the River Aire.[10]

Seal of Ilbert de Lacy.
(Leeds Libraries and Information Services)

The Alien Benedictines of York

York in the 15th Century by Edwin Ridsdale Tate. (The Mansion House and York Museums Trust)
P = Holy Trinity Priory.

This period of turmoil had left the community reeling. Shortly after the Conquest, Ilbert granted the manor of Leeds to Ralph Paynel, another wealthy Norman baron.[11] In 1089 Paynel made a generous gift to the Alien Benedictine monks of Holy Trinity Priory, York. The priory was a dependency of the great French abbey of Marmoutier, at Tours, a wealthy monastery favoured by many members of the Norman elite. Ralph's gift included Leeds parish church with all its income and also the village of Leeds, the 'tithe of the hall', and an additional half carucate of land 'which Reginald had held.' In essence Leeds was now a manor without two of its major sources of income - its church, with its valuable tithes, and the income and labour services of the residents of Kirkgate.

Another charter dated around 1119 confirmed Ralph's gift, those of his sons William and Jordan, together with additional donations made by their vassals and other benefactors. Furthermore it forbade anyone, including hermits, from building a chapel or any kind of oratory within the bounds of the parish without the permission of the Prior and Convent, and no one else was to minister to the parishioners of Leeds or receive their benefactions.

This guaranteed that St Peter's remained the religious centre of the parish, used every Sunday for worship and for the great events of life – baptism, marriage and death. The priory also retained the right to appoint the vicar. As Leeds prospered the income derived from the tithes, Leeds parish church and the village of Kirkgate rose to become critically important to Holy Trinity, providing over half its annual income.[12]

The peasant families of Kirkgate were now free from all feudal obligations formerly owed to the lord of the manor of Leeds. Above all they no longer had the heavy obligation to labour without payment for part of the week on the Paynel's home farm. They now had little agricultural land of their own to cultivate, other than the ground surrounding their Kirkgate farmhouses, and so instead took up any trade or craft they could turn their hand to; many found weaving cloth a useful form of by-employment. They were now also free from the obligation to have their corn ground at the corn mill of the manor of Leeds; remarkably this significant loss of income to the miller was to remain a thorny issue for centuries!

The dramatic changes brought about by the gift of Kirkgate to the Alien Benedictines initially must have greatly disrupted the lives of the people of Kirkgate but the fact that for the next 450 years the church and original village of Kirkgate remained in the hands of this French religious organization seems to have provided a stability within which the inhabitants were able to prosper.[13]

4

What did Ralph Paynel give to the Alien Benedictine monks of York?

In the bottom right corner of the picture overleaf we see the most important part of the manor — the manorial hall and church enclosures. This complex had probably been constructed in the Anglo-Saxon period and was carefully sited on the river terrace near the confluence of the River Aire and Sheepscar Beck and on the edge of the marshy ground to the east. It provided a safe haven for the lord of the manor and the early Christians who worshipped in the church. This small wooden church (**1**), with its south facing door, stood within a large ditched enclosure. To its left we see a second ditched enclosure. This was home to the thegns who controlled the area, who at some time in the Anglo-Scandinavian period had built a wooden hall (**2**) and associated buildings there. It was their distinctive crosses and grave covers which adorned the churchyard. The monks of Holy Trinity were to use this ancient Anglo-Scandinavian manor house as their administrative centre. These buildings stand at the end of the trackway which we see leading from the main fording point of the River Aire (**3**) at the bottom left of the picture.[14] This major route way to York was later named 'The Calls'.

The church was the centre of worship for the vast parish of Leeds and its graveyard provided a final resting place for parishioners. Money was needed to support the upkeep of the church and the sustenance of the priest and so parishioners were required to give one-tenth of their income to the church. This came in the form of the great tithes of corn and hay, and the small tithes of livestock, wool and non-cereal crops.[15] Just below the manorial enclosure is the vast tithe barn (**4**) where all this produce was stored. The monks were to hold their manor courts in the tithe barn, a fact which is still recalled today in the name of High Court Lane which ran beside it.

Running diagonally up to the left from the churchyard we see Kirkgate itself, the village street. At this time there were rectangular tofts of land on each side bounded by ditches,

hedges or fences. Here we see the timber-framed cottages of the villagers with their yards and small allotments where chickens, pigs and perhaps a cow were kept.[16] Meadowland (**5**) hugged the riverside below The Calls and provided vital winter fodder for the animals. To the left of the picture we can also see areas of pasture for sheep and cattle. Sheep provided fleeces, meat and milk, while cows produced milk, meat and leather, and oxen were needed to pull the village ploughs.

The monks were also given some arable land, particularly to the north of Kirkgate, where we see it bounded by a stream which ran into Sheepscar Beck on the right. This land, formerly part of the network of large open fields of the manor of Leeds, was divided into distinct ridge and furrow plough-land strips. This is where the villagers grew wheat, rye or barley and vegetable crops. Opposite the parish church was an area of woodland and an orchard (**6**) that provided fruit for the inhabitants.[17] On the far left of the picture, running north from the river ford across the enclosure, we see the track which today we know as Call Lane. Taking a dog-leg at its junction with Kirkgate, travellers could proceed northwards to Harewood and the ford across the River Wharfe.

The Manor of Kirkgate in 1089 (PB) overleaf. Due to the chance survival of an eighteenth century map which delineated the bounds of the manor of Kirkgate, it is possible to identify quite precisely the physical extent of the land Ralph Paynel gave to the Holy Trinity Priory in 1089. Shapes of fields and enclosures and even individual tofts often remain written in the landscape for many centuries and by a minute examination and analysis of maps and property deeds dating from 1560 to the late Victorian period we have been able to reconstruct the physical subdivisions within the manor of Kirkgate at this time. Combining this evidence with additional evidence from a range of medieval and later sources, it has been possible to produce the picture overleaf of what the manor would have looked like in 1089. Inevitably some elements of this are conjectural but the internal field and plots boundaries seem certain and interestingly the overall form is consistent with what present-day scholars would expect of a medieval village of this date.

KIRKGATE

CALL LANE

THE CALLS

3

4

Key

1 Church
2 Hall
3 Fording Point
4 Tithe Barn
5 Meadowland
6 Woodland and Orchard

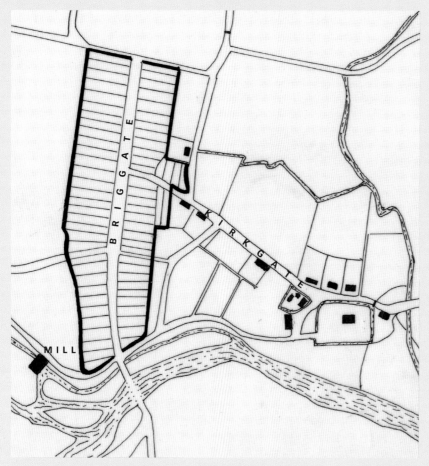

Reconstruction Plan of Leeds in 1207. (Steven Burt)

New Neighbours

When Ralph Paynel gave the parish church and Kirkgate and its manor house to the Priory of Holy Trinity in 1089, he must have transferred the administrative base of the manor of Leeds to the new Norman fortified 'castle' site to the extreme west of the settlement (today occupied by the Scarbrough Taps public house). Just over a hundred years later when Maurice de Gant inherited his great-great-grandfather's manor of Leeds, he must have cursed the generosity of his ancestor and the consequent diminution of his manorial income. Like so many noblemen of the period Maurice sought to create a manorial borough or new town in Leeds, separate from the old village of Leeds, which he hoped would become a successful market and generate additional income for him.[18] Leeds was a promising location for a new market town. It was an important transhipment point for river traffic, and road traffic across the Pennines and to and from York, Pontefract, Wakefield, Harewood, Knaresborough, Skipton and Rothwell would also pass this way. In 1207, using his grandmother's surname, Paynel, Maurice summoned over fifteen important local noblemen to witness the granting of the charter for his new borough.

The villagers of Kirkgate must have watched in amazement as a band of workmen began to peg out a broad new street leading directly north from just above the main fording point of the River Aire to the southern edge of the Woodhouse field system. Briggate, as it was later known, was ninety perches long (1485 feet). The workmen carefully measured and marked the boundaries of thirty-five burgage plots on the west side of the street and thirty on the east, these varying in depth from ten to eighteen perches. Even the awkward pieces of land at Kirkgate End, which were not part of the Alien Benedictine's manor of Kirkgate, and formed a wedge between the old village and the new market street, were pegged out to accommodate additional plots. Altogether Maurice created over sixty half acre plots which he hoped would soon be occupied by skilled craftsmen attracted by the modest annual rent of sixteen pence, eight pence due at Whitsun and eight pence at Martinmas. He encouraged people to build houses and workshops at their own expense, attracted by the burghal liberties that came with holding this land. Above all the charter granted personal freedom to each of the individual tenants in that, unlike tenants of the manor of Leeds, they were free from the reviled feudal obligation to work for part of the week without payment on the lord's own agricultural land. In addition he gave them each an allotment of half an acre at some distance from the new town at what became known as Burmantofts or 'burgagemen's tofts', where they could grow vegetables and keep animals.

Nevertheless, Maurice required each burgess to attend the lord's court where the affairs of the manor were regulated and 'bake in my oven according to custom'.[19] He hoped that this monopoly would bring in more revenue in addition to that gained from the lease of the watermill at Mill Hill, where everyone in the manor of Leeds had to have their corn ground. He duly ordered the construction of a new court house and a bakehouse or manorial oven.

The villagers of Kirkgate must have envied their new 'free' neighbours in the town to some extent but the knowledge that these burgesses were burdened with the additional cost of having their baking done in the lord's oven and their corn ground at the lord's mill would have counterbalanced this. As the Prior's tenants they

The Medieval Court House and Bakehouse, c.1438. (PB)

labour plus 12d to hire the adjoining garden of John Arosmyth in which the carpenters and other workmen could work. Building materials were brought along appalling roads to the construction site. Four wagon loads of timber came from Leeds Park along with five wagon-loads of tiles. Over 1400 laths were transported from the woods of Calverley to cover the main body of the roof. A further five loads of roofing slate came from the quarry at Woodhouse to weigh down the edges in order to prevent possible wind damage. The sum of 2s was paid to a man to gather moss for the roof.

Two sawyers worked hard in Rothwell woods preparing three mould-boards, planking and eaves-boards for use in the bakehouse for which they received 9s, and 4d for a new rope to haul the timber to the saw-pit and preparation area. An additional 12d was paid for transporting the mould-boards from Rothwell. Three carpenters laboured for sixteen days on the repairs to the woodwork. A plasterer used 10 wagonloads of plaster to improve the finish to the walls and John Merston was paid 20s for tiling the hall. The substantial sum of 3s 9d was expended on 700 nails called 'doublespyking', 6s 7d for 4,300 standard nails and 2d for the repair of the lock of the hall door. Once the work had been completed workmen were paid 6d for flooding the ditch that surrounded the hall and 2d for similar fire defences for the bakehouse beneath.[21] Wood as fuel for the oven had initially come from Leeds Park, but the woodland cover was by now depleted. Instead it came much longer distances, from the parks of Roundhay and Rothwell, at 2d a load plus the cost of transport to the town.

had no such restrictions, despite their unfree status.

The bakehouse or oven and court house became key features of the townscape.[20] It is clear that originally the oven and the 'Hall of Pleas' were on separate sites but sometime between 1399 and 1438 a new building comprising both the oven and the court house was constructed to the rear of the plot at the top of Kirkgate, later occupied by the Golden Cock Inn. An alleyway off Kirkgate, today known as Fish Street, was the route along which the firewood was brought. The new combined court house and oven needed constant repair. In 1438 John Hopton, the reeve for the town, had a busy time supervising a major overhaul of the structure. It proved a costly affair with £4 14s 6d expended on materials and

Kirkgate in the Fourteenth and Fifteenth Centuries

Leeds Parish Church, south side, demolished 1838.

Violent Times

Overall the period from 1086 to 1300 was one of increasing prosperity within the parish of Leeds. Income derived from the basic agricultural output was supplemented by substantial monies generated by the wool trade which had expanded since the Cistercian monks had moved to Kirkstall in 1152. Many of the villagers of Kirkgate became skilled clothiers, turning locally produced wool into cloth, and by 1322 enough was being produced to support the construction of a fulling mill where cloth was washed and felted.[22] By 1356 a second fulling mill had been added to keep pace with increasing demand.[23] Rising prosperity gave the Benedictine monks of Holy Trinity the confidence to construct a magnificent new parish church of stone with a fine lead roof and imposing south doorway. This took many years to construct but was complete by 1377. Built in the shape of a cross, with choir, transepts, nave and aisles, it had a tower soaring 96 feet above the crossing. Its layout and impressive scale, 165 feet long, 97 feet wide and 51 foot long nave, gave rise to comments that it was 'built after the manner of a cathedral'.[24] Such a large structure was required to house the growing population of the parish which had risen to about a thousand souls, of whom about 350 to 400 lived on Kirkgate and Briggate.[25]

Despite the construction of chapels of ease in some of the out-townships, like Beeston and (Chapel) Allerton, St Peter's remained the parish's hub of religious activity where the parishioners gathered every Sunday to worship and hear the gossip. Who would have been in the congregation? Nearest to the church were Holy Trinity's own tenants who lived on Kirkgate, The Calls and Call Lane, many deriving their income by weaving and dyeing cloth.

Then there were the elite of the parish, like the de Ledes family of North Hall, near Lady Bridge, and the Scotts of Scott Hall at Potternewton. They lived in fine timber-framed houses complete with impressive halls and stone slate roofs. They were followed in status by the free tenants of the parish, including the Waites family, who held land for money rent and were free from onerous duties on the lord's land. There were the townsfolk from Briggate, skilled clothiers, leather and metal workers, who occupied timber-framed houses with shop or workshop frontages to the street. There was the fuller and his assistants from the fulling mill on the river and the blacksmith from the forge next to the manorial oven.

The remains of a medieval tomb in Leeds Parish Church. The fact that the manor of Leeds was held by an absentee landlord and much of the land in the parish was in the hands of the monks of Holy Trinity Priory and Kirkstall Abbey, meant that there were few families with sufficient wealth to afford such luxurious monuments. This beautiful effigy c.1320, carved in magnesium limestone, depicts a knight wearing a chain mail coif and hauberk, covered by a cloth surtout. The head, which rests on a pillow, is covered by a bassinet with neck-guard. The sword belt, ornamented by roundels, is attached to the scabbard by interlocking thongs. His hands are protected by mail gauntlets and are held in prayer. On his left-hand side he has a shield, the armorial bearings appear to be those of the Manston family of Crossgates. This must have been part of an impressive panelled tomb chest.

There were twenty-four wealthy bondmen who held large farms in Knostrop and Woodhouse and lived in sturdy farmhouses. There were the farm labourers who worked the land and the shepherds who tended the sheep; the skilled women brewers, the quarrymen from Quarry Hill, Woodhouse and Armley, the miners from Carlton Cross, the carters who moved the fruits of the harvest, stone from the nearby quarries, and timber from Rothwell and Seacroft. There was the miller and his workforce from the King's Mills who ground the corn and the baker who ran the manorial oven at Kirkgate End. Finally came the poor cottagers who lived in wattle and daub hovels on small parcels of land scattered throughout the parish, who eked out a meagre living through casual work and supplemented their diet with food they grew on the adjoining plots or the wild fruits gathered on the common land and moors of Leeds, at Woodhouse, Hunslet, Holbeck, Chapel Allerton, Potternewton, Headingley, Wortley, Farnley, Armley, Bramley and Beeston.

There was no seating in the church and members of the congregation had to kneel, stand or prostrate themselves on the cold, stone floor while participating in the service led by the vicar. The service was in Latin and so much of the meaning would be lost on his congregation. It also remained the most important centre of communal activity, the focus of celebrations associated with birth and marriage, a place of prayer for the sick and comfort for the bereaved. It was also the centre for festivities at Christmas, Easter and on the numerous 'holy days', many of which celebrated Catholic saints.

The fact that the manor of Kirkgate was the property of a religious order did not mean it was exempt from the violence of the age. Indeed, no doubt there was some resentment and hostility towards this 'alien' French order of monks who annually took one tenth of the hard-earned produce of the inhabitants of the parish and controlled the manor of Kirkgate. On 26 September 1314 John de Doncastre and Adam de Hoperton were asked to investigate a raid that had taken place on the Priory's property on Kirkgate. Henry de Ledes, Boniface, his brother, John de Bradeford, clerk, William, son of Agnes le Wayt, Hugh le Braythorn, Thomas Hugesman, John le Machun, Elyas, son of John Fissher, Henry, son of Robert Sabyn, Hugh de Tong, Thomas le Charetter, Thomas Rogersman, Robert, son of Thomas de Morewyk and John le Forester were all named as members of the gang. Others were also implicated. In 1314 the Prior claimed that a group of men had 'forcibly entered his manor of Ledes (Kirkgate), by night, broke the gates and doors of his houses, carried away his goods and assaulted Richard de Drynghouse, a fellow-monk of the Priory, and also his men and servants'.[26]

The band that launched the raid included members of two of the wealthiest families in the parish. This was not the only instance of violent behaviour involving the church and the de Ledes and Wayt families as we can see overleaf.

The Leeds Fight

Tower Fechtbuch – The Illuminated Fightbook: Royal Armouries Manuscript I.33.
(Board of Trustees of the Royal Armouries)

On the evening of Sunday, 29 August 1320, William Wayt was killed in a brawl outside the parish church. The attack was a particularly violent one. Roger de North Hall, his sons Roger, Robert, Thomas and Richard, along with Robert Formalt and Robert Rande were accused of his murder. William Wayt's brother, Richard, claimed that Richard de North Hall had grabbed William by the hair while Robert Rande held his right hand. Robert Formalt then struck him on the back of the neck with an ashen stick. The blow left William badly shaken and nursing a broken collar bone. At that moment Thomas came forward, grabbed William firmly by the left shoulder before his brother, Robert, using 'a certain sword made in Cologne', delivered a mortal blow to the right arm. Major criminal offences being the concern of the royal courts, members of the 'de North Hall gang' were rounded up by the King's Marshall, who decided that there was a case to answer. John Travers, Alexander de Ledes, William de Scargill, John de Calverley, Robert de Scargill and William the Forester escorted the accused men to the courts of King Edward II.

The story then took an unusual twist. Richard Wayt failed to appear at the hearing and all of the prisoners were released on bail and were ordered to reappear before the king in a month's time. When they did appear the story they told the coroner, George de Thornton, was rather different.

Gang members claimed that there had been a dispute between William de Wayt and Robert de Ledes over a game they had been playing at lunchtime, just prior to the Sunday service. Neighbours had intervened in the argument and both men entered the parish church carrying their swords and bucklers. After vespers had been sung, William Wayt left the church with Thomas, his page, and John de Manston. They lingered by the church stile waiting for Robert to leave. When he came out members of the congregation encouraged him to go home immediately. William's friends John de Manston goaded Robert who, realising he was in peril, tried to re-enter the church but the clergy and some parishioners closed the door fearing that the church may be put under an interdict if a crime was committed on its premises. Robert wedged his back against the wall and turned to William who tried to hit him with his sword. Robert defended himself with his buckler and then struck out at William. This successful blow to William's right arm proved fatal. John de Manston, Thomas Nesant and Robert de Wayt, who was a chaplain at St Peter's, threw Robert de Ledes onto the ground and launched several blows to his head and body, before leaving him for dead in the ditch that surrounded the church. Richard and Thomas de Ledes came looking for their brother and, on finding him 'speechless and moving no limb', carried him to the manor house of their father, located near Lady Bridge. Their father was stunned and at first refused to let them in. Robert's sword and buckler, worth 18d, were subsequently confiscated and he was taken to London where he was imprisoned in the Marshalsea gaol awaiting the judgment of the royal court. Robert's family and friends argued that he had killed William Wayt in self-defence, something that Richard Wayt did not deny. Proceedings dragged on but eventually, on 31 July 1321, Edward II ordered Robert's release. The Earl of Pembroke witnessed the pardon but it was not until the 20 November that he was finally set free.[27]

Men of Money and Piety

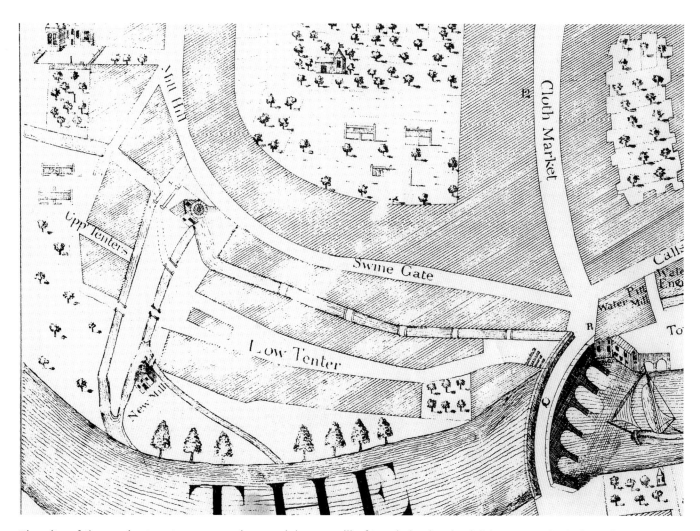

The site of the ancient water-powered manorial corn mill of Leeds is clearly visible on Cossins' Plan of 1726. There had been a mill here since Anglo-Scandinavian times and it is mentioned in the Domesday Book of 1086. Over time a complex water-management system had developed including the construction of substantial dams and goits. The right to grind corn was a jealously guarded and lucrative monopoly. Tenants of Holy Trinity Priory were free to grind their corn wherever they wished, much to the annoyance of the Lords of the Manor of Leeds and the lessees of the manorial mill.

The huge impact of the Black Death (1349) and civil wars in the fourteenth century must have rocked to the core the people of the Parish of Leeds, but by the end of the century it was clear that the local economy had grown.[28] By 1400 Roger de Ledes, knight, dominated the town, leasing from the lord of the manor of Leeds the water-mill, rents from the burgesses of Briggate, the common oven and toll of the market and fairs for the very considerable sum of £30 3s 4d. This was at a time when a carpenter earned around 5d a day, a labourer perhaps 4d or around £4 a year overall.[29]

In 1430 Thomas Clarell became Vicar of Leeds and ministered well to the needs of his parishioners until his death in 1469.[30] In 1453 William Scot of Potter Newton had donated a parcel of land to the east of Vicar Lane, formerly William Rivause's, to Robert Neville and Thomas Clarell, on which to build a manse with gardens.

Clarell was also a great benefactor of St Peter's, adorning the chancel with fine paintings and founding the chantry of St Katherine the Virgin and Martyr, within the south transept of the church.[31] Such foundations were very popular in the fifteenth century, often named after the donor's favourite saint. A certificate, issued by Robert, Archbishop of York, allowed a priest to be employed to fulfil special chantry duties including the singing of masses to the soul of the deceased donor.[32] From the Chantry Surveys it is known that Clarell wished the priest to pray for the soul of King Edward IV, Queen Elizabeth, his own soul and that of 'all Cristen soules and to do dyvyne service'.[33] The chapel was founded in June 1489, twenty years after Clarell's death. It was adorned with goods, ornaments and plate.

The chief trustee of this new foundation was Richard Neville, knight, one of the wealthiest men in the district, with land at Liversedge and Hunslet. It seems likely that under his supervision a fine timber-framed house was built on Kirkgate for the new chantry priest who also catered for the spiritual needs of sick and poor Christians housed in the hospitium next door. One of the common duties of a chantry priest was to teach the young and it is highly likely that this took place in his home on Kirkgate until 1547.[34] Fortunately the location of both the chantry priest's house and hospitium can be pinpointed accurately as Thoresby states that the First White Cloth Hall was built on their site.

◄ *Interior of Leeds Parish Church by J. N. Rhodes c.1835. View of the north transept with its fine medieval stonework and tracery window which had been built at great expense by masons working for the Alien Benedictines of Holy Trinity Priory, York. (Leeds Library and Information Services)*

◄ *Around 1500 the upper chamber of a timber-framed house, possibly that of the chantry priest, (later nos. 103-4 Kirkgate) was richly decorated with an exceptionally fine series of wall paintings. This detail is on a piece of timber discovered in the charred remains of the building behind Hill's Furnishings, which caught fire in December 2015. It shows the heads of a number of fabulous creatures, perhaps a depiction of the mouth of Hell. (Redrawn PB)*

The Rise of the Clothiers: Tudor Kirkgate

On 11 December 1536 the Prior and ten priests surrendered Holy Trinity Priory, valued at £169 9s 0d per annum, to Leigh and Layton, Henry VIII's commissioners. The Reformation removed at a stroke over four centuries of stability that had been enjoyed by their tenants.

In 1545 some Kirkgate properties were included in a crown sale of former monastic lands to William Ramsden of Longley, gentleman, and Edward Hoppey junior of Halifax, clothier, for the total sum of £1066 4s 1⅛d. They were acting as agents for many powerful men who were the intended purchasers. A deed of partition dated 13 July 1545 left the Kirkgate property in the hands of Ramsden, a successful clothier from Elland, near Halifax. Unfortunately some part of the complex series of deals went sour and he was unable to make the final payment in full.[35] Nevertheless this grant gives us for the first time some detailed information about the structure of the manor of Kirkgate. Twenty-four properties are referred to including Bentley House, Franke House and Lez Garners which were all held by a widow named Elizabeth Fentyman, plus a cottage next to 'lez mylles' in the occupation of Thomas Key. The grant also lists thirteen cottages with gardens, three cottages with crofts and four individual cottages.

In addition there was still arable land and meadow within the bounds of the manor: reference is made to arable land in lez Holmes, a piece of meadow called Kyrkeynge (Kirk Ings), two acres of meadow called Litle Lecke, and another two acres occupied by Widow Fentyman. Clearly there was a shortage of trees — a fascinating detail given is that 'The trees growing in the hedges about the seyd lands wyll barely suffice for stakes for hedgebood [the right to take wood from the common land] to repayre and maynteyne the scyd hedges and fences.'

Certain family names are mentioned that become familiar in the future development of Leeds, those of Lupton, Cowper, Arthington, Marshall, Sykes, Harrison, Kirke, Atkinson and Frank.[36] Many of these families would have been dependent on the cloth trade, their homes a hive of activity, where they produced Northern dozens, broadcloths and coverlets for the local, national and international markets, in direct competition with the traditional cloth-making centres of York and Beverley whose powerful guilds dominated the industry.

The period 1400 to 1550 had been one of great expansion in the textile trade. The population of the parish grew to around 3,000 and the number of fulling mills, dye-vats and tenter frames continued to grow apace providing the necessary facilities to support the manufacture of cloth. The Kirkgate clothiers continued to grow in wealth, skill and stature; free of any guild restrictions they could produce high quality cloth at lower prices than their urban rivals. In 1561, one writer bewailed the state of trade in York:

> The cause of the decay of the …weavers and loomes for the woollen [cloth] within the sayd cite as I doe understand and learne is the lak of cloth making in the sayd cite as was in old tyme accustomed, which is nowe encreased and used in the townes of Halyfax, Leedes and Wakefield. For that not only the comodytie of the water-mylnes is ther nigh at hande, but also the poore folke as speynners, carders, and other necessary work-folkes for the sayd webbying, may ther besyde ther hand labor, have rye, fyre, and other relief good cheape, which is in this citie very deare and wantyng.[37]

The men of York felt that the best way to ensure that only its citizens could enjoy the right to manufacture these products was by seeking a monopoly of production through an Act of Parliament. This was duly obtained in 1543 and particular reference was made to the manufacture of coverlets which were being made outside the city by those without skill, stock, or knowledge 'to the great slander of true cloth-making'.[38] The statute proved impossible to enforce and the clothiers of Kirkgate continued to prosper and grow in number.

The typical clothier combined cloth-making with small-scale farming activities; having a field or two with his cottage, growing food and keeping a few animals. As the textile industry prospered so did the residents of Kirkgate.

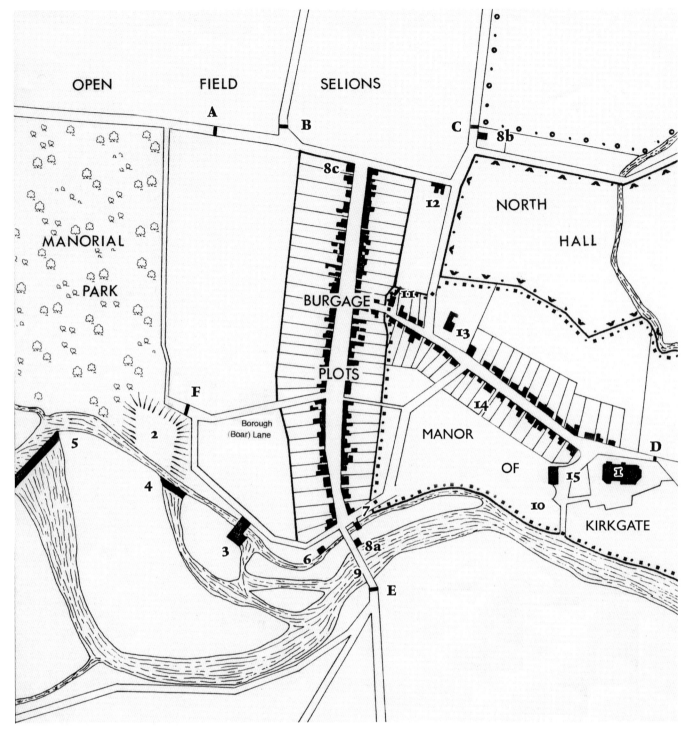

The Town of Leeds in 1500. (Steven Burt)

Key

1. St. Peter's – the parish church
2. Castelhyll – site of the former fortified Leeds manor house
3. Manorial Corn Mill
4. Bondman Dam
5. High Dam
6. Fulling Mill
7. Fulling Mill
8. Chantry Chapels:
   a St. Mary's on the Bridge
   b Lady Chapel
   c Sir William Eures' Chapel
9. Leeds Bridge
10. Tithe Barn
11. Manorial Oven with Hall of Pleas above
12. Rockley Hall
13. The Vicarage
14. The Hospitium
15. Kirkgate Manor House

The Bars – the boundaries of the medieval town

A Burley Bar
B Woodhouse Bar
C North Bar
D East or York Bar
E South Bar
F West Bar

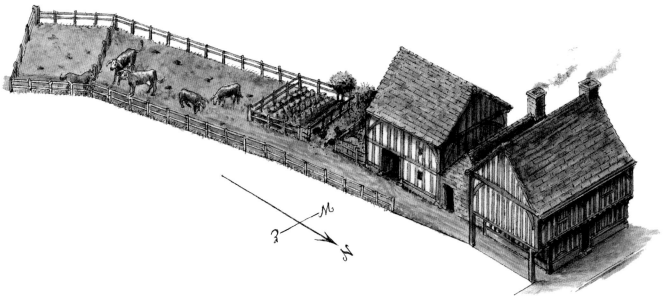

Pawson's house and toft. (PB)

John Pawson is an excellent example of a Kirkgate clothier. He was married with only one child, a son called Christopher, but his extended family of six brothers and two sisters were of critical importance. The Pawsons were long-established in the parish and one branch of the family had been residents in Kirkgate from at least the early fifteenth century.[39] When he died in 1576 he was a man of substance with house servants and three apprentices, who worked on site but lodged elsewhere. His wife and son inherited £69 18s 5d but John had also given large sums in legacies to his extended family. His mother, brothers, sisters, nephews, nieces and his god-children all benefited and, coupled with his funeral expenses, mortuary, money to the poor and a donation towards the repair of the highways, a further £23 4s 8d was disbursed.

On 5 February 1576 four of Pawson's neighbours, George Cowper, Lawrence Awstropp, John Mawson and William Lightfoot, all 'clothiers of Kirkgate', drew up an inventory which provides a special insight into the contents of his home and the lifestyle of a Tudor clothier. His timber-framed house fronted the street. In the yard to the rear was a dye-house or 'lead-house' where the cloth was dyed. Inside was a single lead bowl under which a fire could be lit, four tubs and a series of baskets. There was a timber-framed barn where he kept his horse, a hackney saddle and a pack saddle for goods. In the yard were piles of un-threshed barley, hay, grass, wood, coal and 'sawne bordes' plus two tenter heads and a rope used in the stretching of fulled cloth. There was also a section of open ground where he tended a vegetable plot and kept his horse, two cows, three young oxen, a couple of pigs, a cockerel and three hens.

Pawson's inventory provides a unique insight into the methods of cloth production in Kirkgate in the Tudor period. The room-by-room list of all the 'goodes, corne, cattel [and] moveables', considered alongside the accurately surveyed plans of the Pawson property made in the late nineteenth century, enable their contents to be visually recreated with a high degree of accuracy. However, it must be understood that the inventory was taken just after Pawson's death, when his business had ceased, and some artefacts in the barns and back yard had been moved into the house itself to protect them from theft. This explains why a hack, two axes, two hatchets, a spade, two shovels, two shod forks, two iron forks and three sacks of barley appear in the office house, completely out of context. Similarly a scray, a wooden frame like a short, broad, ladder with very close-set rungs used to drain freshly-dyed wool in the lead-house, had been brought into the loom-house.

Pawson was a skilled clothier and, in addition to manufacturing standard lengths of woollen cloth called 'northern dozens', he produced high-value coverlets. This canny businessman supplemented his sizeable income by farming agricultural land in Woodhouse, renting out three tenements in Marsh Lane and through money lending, which was common practice at the time.

Cross-section through Pawson's house showing the contents of the office-cum-kitchen and the chamber above. The front door on to Kirkgate is on the right. (PB)

Pawson's modest house, a copyhold property, was a hive of activity, comprising four rooms: an office-cum-kitchen, a parlour, a chamber and a shop/loom-house. You entered from the street into the office-cum-kitchen, the only heated room in the house, the fire burning brightly in an impressive iron range complete with a pair of racks and three spits. To the side were various cooking implements and a selection of tools used to keep the fire going. This room provided the ideal opportunity for Pawson to impress his visitors through a fine display of brass pots, expensive pans, twenty-two pewter dishes, twenty saucers, fine pottery, two salts and three brass-like candlesticks. His furniture too was more extensive and of better quality than many of his neighbours, comprising a long table, a cupboard, two chairs, two buffet stools and other smaller items, additional comfort being provided by ten cushions. In this room he kept his clothing, a girdle, a dagger and a purse containing sixteen pence. Three sacks of barley had been moved here for safe keeping.

Above the office-cum-kitchen was the chamber where he stored the vast quantities of white and coloured wool that he used in the manufacture of the cloth. In the picture we see only a fraction of the amount he had stockpiled. Here he kept the butter for greasing the shuttle as it flew from one end of the loom to the other, and alum, the name given to the double salts of aluminium and potassium, a critical compound used as a fixative in the process of dyeing wool. The items on the shelves in the middle of the room are wool combs, which, when heated, were used to remove any short fibres from long staple wool in order to make worsted yarn. This was then used in the production of the finest quality worsted cloth that commanded the best prices and had traditionally been produced in York and Beverley under the strict regulation of the cloth guilds.

To the left are two large arks that contained the barley, rye and wheat with which to make flour for baking. In the centre of the room are the various troughs and tubs that were used to make the dough for their bread.

Cross-section through Pawson's house showing the contents of the parlour and the shop/loom-house above. Kirkgate is on the right. The view looks west, with the kitchen range seen through the central doorway. (PB)

Returning to the ground floor, we enter the parlour which also doubled as a bedroom. It was only heated by leaving open the door to the adjoining kitchen. It also acted as a store-room for food including flitches of salt beef which provided the family with tasty meat throughout the year. At the time of his death, Pawson's mother, wife and son were alive. The couple occupied one bed and either his mother or son the other. Draped over both beds are fine quality chequered worsted coverlets that Pawson had made. In the cupboard and chests were stored towels, linen sheets, blankets, pillows and covers. Pawson's neighbours noted a cupboard containing five silver spoons worth fifteen shillings and thirty shillings in cash. Other valuable assets were the seven flitches of salt beef that hung from the ceiling.

Above, in the shop and loom-house, were found the tools necessary for producing cloth including a spinning wheel and his loom. As we have already noted the workforce comprised at least Pawson, his son and three apprentices working in his Kirkgate house, but to provide sufficient yarn to serve his loom he had to put out large quantities of raw wool to spinners working elsewhere. They still held five stone of wool and ten stone of yarn, valued at £8 5s at his death. Hanging on the wall at either side of the window were six pairs of shears plus a shear-board and two pairs of irons. These were used in the finishing process to give the cloth its final finish after it had been washed and felted in one of the fulling mills that abutted the River Aire and then stretched on the tenter frames that were located in the south-facing fields behind the property. John also held a large quantity of unsold stock - 'twenty-one dozens' of finished pieces of cloth worth eighty five shillings.

Finally the inventory reveals that he was owed £18 19s 4d of 'good debtes' plus some 'desperat debtes' which he had little prospect of collecting.[40]

Cloth-making in Leeds

The process of cloth-making commenced with the purchase of wool from a wool-merchant. This would be the 15 stone of white wool that is listed in the chamber, most probably wrapped up in pack-sheets. From here it would be beaten and teased to remove any grit and loosen the locks before being dyed in a large boiler called a lead set up in the lead-house. Baskets and tubs were used to hold separate batches of dry or wet wool, and the scray to drain it before being dried, probably wrapped in pack-sheets, and stored in the chamber. There was the 41 stone of coloured wool 'dyed in the wool' listed in the inventory.

The presence of 'certeyne happynge garne' in the lead-house is of particular interest, since happings were coverlets for beds, proving that these were being made in Leeds, perhaps from wool dyed in the yarn. From the lead-house the wool was stored in the chamber, sent out to be carded and spun, and returned in hanks to the loom-shop. Here the 'wheel' was a spinning wheel used as a bobbin-winder to take half of the yarn from the hank onto the bobbins, these being transferred to a 'creel' from where multiple yarns were drawn off to form a warp, the longitudinal threads of the cloth. This was done by passing them between rows of horizontal pegs set into two posts a few yards apart called bartrees. The complete warp was then removed, a certain number of yarns arranged between the pegs of a long wooden frame called a raddle to spread them out evenly, and wound onto a long roller called a beam that fitted on the back of the loom. Alternate yarns passed above and below a pair of 'premes' or preems, 'white wands… for the opening of the yarn so that each thread may pass clearly through the reed', which are now called lease-rods. The yarns were then threaded through the eyes of healds, which raised and lowered them alternately to leave a gap called a 'shed', through the comb-like 'reed' that beat the warp or cross-threads into place, and onto a second roller called a cloth-beam at the front of the loom. Using the wheel once more, the remaining half of the yarn was wound onto narrow bobbins called 'pirns' and fitted inside the shuttle, ready for the loom. As the weaver used treadles to operate the healds, opening 'sheds' for the shuttle to pass through and the reed to consolidate the cloth, a 'northern dozen' was gradually formed, a piece of cloth measuring 1¾ yards (63 inches) wide by 13 yards long.

When completed, this 'piece' would be soaked in urine on a stone floor, this liquid combining with the wool's natural grease to form a soap. The piece would then be carried to the fulling mill, where the power of the river was utilised to operate large wooden hammers to pound the cloth until its fibres had felted together, so that individual yarns could no longer be seen on its slightly shaggy surface. From the mill Pawson would take his piece to the tenter-ground (later occupied by the Third White Cloth Hall) to be stretched and dried on his tenter-frames, his 'ii tenter heades, tenter Rope' being stored in his Kirkgate outbuildings.

George Walker (1781-1856) of Killingbeck Hall painted this scene of spinning and hank-winding c. 1814.

Extract from Buck's 1720 Prospect of Leeds, showing tentering and willeying with willow rods to remove the dust and break up the locks of raw wool.

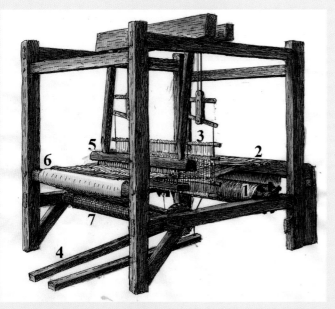

◄ *On a typical handloom the longitudinal warp threads passed from the warp beam (1), through a pair of lease rods (2) and the healds that raised and lowered alternate threads (3) by means of treadles (4). Each consecutive weft thread was beaten into place by the reed (5) to form cloth, its width being maintained by a temple (6) before it was wound on to the cloth beam (7). (PB)*

Detail of Lodge's Prospect c. 1680 showing the tenter frames with the fulling mills behind. ▼

Once dry, the piece returned to the loom-shop and had its shagge 'nap' raised up using the heads of Fullers' teazles. A long narrow table called a 'shearboard' protected by its 'shearborde coverage' was set end-on to a window, and one end of the piece stretched along it. One of the four sets of 'walker shcares', now known as cropping shears, was rested on one selvedge. These shears were huge, around 4 feet long, with a pair of broad razor-sharp blades joined by a 'bentt' or almost circular iron bow. As one blade rested on the cloth, probably weighed down with the 'iiii Fresynge stones', the other trimmed the nap to an even height, an extremely skilful process, one mistake ruining the whole piece. Since the bow of the shears was so strong as to be unmanageable if attempted to be used solely by the hands, the 'viii course of handles' was essential. Each had a binding to fit onto one blade, and another to link it to a vertical handle on the other, this providing the required leverage and control for every cut. Since there is no mention of

a cloth-press in the inventory it appears that the finished cloths were then rolled up, ready to be displayed over the parapet of Leeds Bridge at the weekly cloth market for sale to the merchants.

Pawson's inventory confirms our understanding of the working practices of Leeds' Elizabethan clothiers. At this period they were undertaking most of the processes within their own homes, only putting out the carding, spinning and fulling stages. The production of broad cloths and kerseys boomed as their price was so competitive and undercut the competition in the West Country, Kent and Worcester. They were sent by carrier or shipped from York or Selby to London. Yet their fame spread and soon there was demand from Holland and Germany. The separation of role between the weavers who produced the cloth only to the fulling stage, and the merchants who purchased it, finished it, and arranged its national and international sales was still to be developed.[41]

Chantries, Court Houses and Corn Milling

Kirkgate was to directly experience the effects of the Tudor monarchs' reforms in the church and local government particularly those of the last three-quarters of the sixteenth century. Following his appropriation of monastic land and assets, in 1546 Henry VIII had granted 'The Rectory of St Peter's at Leedes' including the tithes of the parish, to the Dean and Chapter of Christ Church, Oxford, so the church and parish had new proprietors.[42] In another radical change in 1547 his son, Edward VI, suppressed the chantries whose priests had not only prayed for the souls of the dead but often served as schoolmasters for a few fortunate boys in their locality.

In some recompense for closing down and appropriating the wealth of the chantries, Edward encouraged the founding (or perhaps perpetuation) of grammar schools. Many schools were founded with monies from the former chantries. The last priest of the Chantry of St Katherine at the parish church was William Sheffeald, who had been appointed by Sir John Neville in 1500 and resided in the chantry priest's house in Kirkgate until 1547. Aware that King Edward was adamant that such institutions were to be abolished and all related property confiscated, he pre-empted the king's action and on 6 March 1547 surrendered all his copyhold land in Leeds to Sir John Neville and fifteen others to generate an income for him until his death. This ploy was successful but the chantry and also 'a tenement late in the tenure of William Sheffelde, late incumbent there' were confiscated, the king granting Sheffeald a pension of just over £4 per annum as some consolation.[43] Almost certainly to perpetuate the teaching of children, in his will dated 6 July 1552, he bequeathed the income from his property 'for the use and for findings Sustentation and Livings for one honest Substantial learned man to teach and instruct freely for ever all such Younge Schollars Youthes and Children as shall come and resort to him from time to time to be taught and informed in such a School house as shall be founded erected and buylded by the Paryshioners of the sayd Towns and Parishe of Leedes'. This was the long-term endowment which resulted in the foundation of Leeds Grammar School.[44]

Another change which was to have an impact on Kirkgate was the innovations in local government under the Tudors. Until the fifteenth century it was primarily the manorial authorities which oversaw and regulated the life and commercial activities of the manor; in the Tudor period increasingly it was a range of unpaid parish and county officials – such as churchwardens, overseers of the poor, surveyors of highways and constables – under the supervision of Justices of the Peace, who became responsible for local affairs and services. The tasks and responsibilities of the Justices themselves extended to overseeing the maintenance of law and order to having vagabonds flogged, deciding the paternity of illegitimate children, apprenticing children, fixing wages, regulating the price of corn and other foods, and many other social and commercial matters.

This rise in the important role of the Justices of the Peace and their functions is highlighted by the continuing story of the court house and manorial oven in Kirkgate — it was no longer adequate for the needs of the growing town or suitable for the dignity of the landed gentry who sat on the bench. In a petition to Queen Elizabeth in November 1598 a Robert Littlewood made her officials aware that 'the Sessions of the Peace within the West Rydinge of the Countie of York were yearly holden at Leedes within her Majesties Honour of Pontefract in a roome beinge directly over the Comon Ovens and furnaces there, which by the smoke and heate of the same ovens and furnaces dayly ascendinge into the said Courthouse, is very inconvenient, noysom and greate hindrance to such as were to exercise her Majestie's service there'.

In exchange for the granting of certain privileges to him, Littlewood offered to build in the middle of Briggate in replacement 'a convenient moote hall and twoe chamber rooms for juryies and jurers for the Service of her Majestie'. Though Littlewood's scheme did not proceed, the writing was on the wall; in 1615 a new Moot Hall was built in Briggate and the judicial functions of the bakehouse in Kirkgate were at an end.[45]

The medieval church and the gabled Tudor and Stuart houses of Kirkgate from a wood engraving of 1733. (Redrawn by PB)

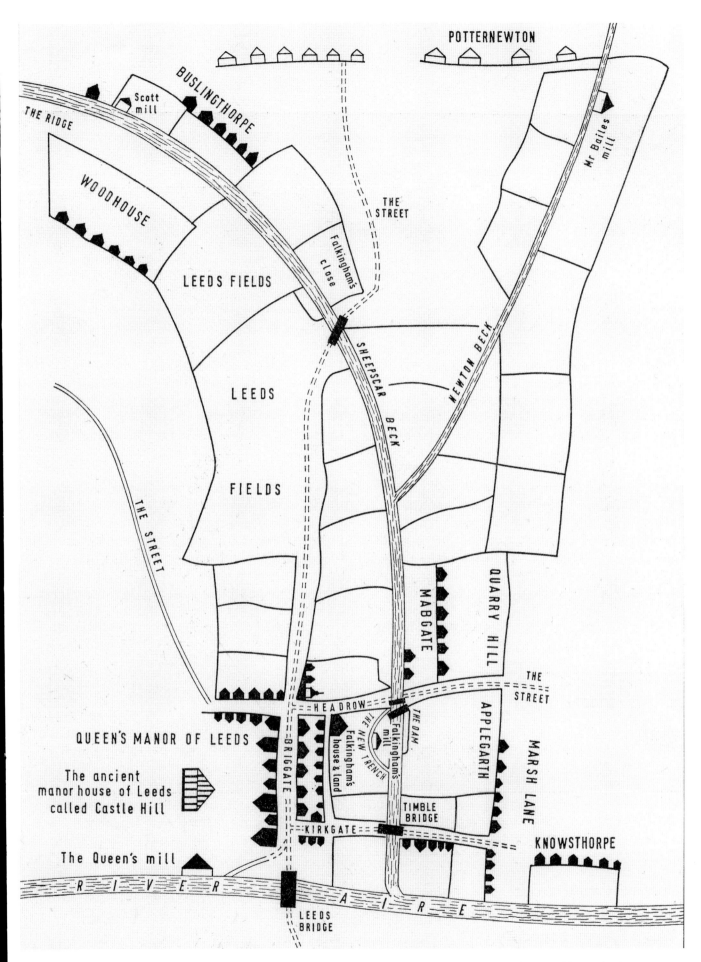

This very first plan of Leeds dated c.1560 was used in a law-suit in which Thomas Lyndley and his wife, farmers (lessees) of the manor of Leeds (Queen's) Mills, complained that Thomas Falkingham, owner of a new corn mill on Sheepscar Beck at Mill Garth, was illegally taking business away from them. It shows the location of the two mills and their relationship to the village of Kirkgate and the town based on Briggate. The tenants of the manor of Kirkgate were later involved in disputes about where they ground their corn. (Thoresby Society, X, 1899)

Without doubt the inhabitants of Kirkgate prospered in the second half of the sixteenth century, John Pawson being a prime example. Indeed it seems likely that their number doubled in that period. This is confirmed by surviving legal papers dating from 1597 to 1600 which tell us that there were now over fifty houses within the manor and even lists the names of the heads of each household. It also introduces us to some of its important people and the tensions between them. The documents arose from a dispute between John Lyndley, the lessee of the manor of Leeds corn mill, and William Bainton, the miller of Hunslet, about whether the residents of the manor of Kirkgate had an obligation to grind their corn at the Leeds mill.[46]

As we have seen, the residents of the manor of Leeds had the feudal obligation to grind their corn at the Leeds mill and indeed were not allowed to consume flour which had not been ground there. The miller of Leeds was loathed by the tenants of the manor of Leeds because of the exorbitant rates he charged for grinding corn and the strong suspicion that the flour he ground had been adulterated. The residents of Kirkgate, on the other hand, had no such obligation, a fact which had been beyond dispute when the influential prior of Holy Trinity had been the lord of the manor. The residents of Kirkgate chose instead to use Hunslet Mill and Scott Mill at Buslingthorpe where it cost considerably less to have their corn ground.

By the late 1590s, when memories of the Holy Trinity era had begun to fade and the location of the boundary between Kirkgate and the manor of Leeds had become blurred, John Lyndley decided to chance his arm and claim that all the residents of Kirkgate were obliged to grind their corn at the Leeds mill. A ruling in his favour would bring him a substantial number of new customers and increase his income. It was worth a gamble! At his request the Queen's Court of Exchequer appointed a 'Special Commission' to look into the matter. The four commissioners were distinguished local men — Ralph Beeston, Thomas Bland, William Dyneley, who all had the status of bearing coats of arms, and Francis Wood 'gentleman'. More significantly for us the transcripts of evidence taken from witnesses bring Kirkgate and the people of the time to life.[47]

The commissioners summoned a jury of local men who had an intimate knowledge of the manor of Kirkgate in the hope that they could provide them with a definitive list of tenants who had the right to grind their corn wherever they chose. The witnesses called included Samuel

Casson of Leeds, gentleman, the Deputy Steward of her majesty for the manor of Leeds Kirkgate aged 36 years 'or thereabouts'; Edward Iles of Holbeck, clothier, aged 38 years; William Wilson, aged 53, a shereman (a cropper) and constable of Leeds Kirkgate; Thomas Wilson, a 37 year old yeoman of Leeds, who had gathered rents of the Kirkgate properties in his capacity as a deputy to Thomas Sandwith, one of the Collectors of Her Majesty's Revenues of the Exchequer; John Wood of Birstall, yeoman aged 37, and Robert Banes, yeoman of Knowstrop aged 60 (these latter two presumably local farmers with a knowledge matters relating to corn production and handling); and Robert Roberts of Leeds; a tailor aged 59. The jury eventually listed 56 people who retained this right (see the footnote for their names) but not even they totally agreed with each other![48]

Samuel Casson the Deputy Steward of the manor of Kirkgate, thought that there were also 'certain cottages under the Call bancke' that should be included. William Wilson believed that all the people living in Leeds Kirkgate, apart from Richard Brodeley, William Sharp and William Waddesworth, owed suit at the Court of Leeds Kirkgate. As constable he had known 'all the said inhabitants (except before excepted) do their suits at the Court of Leedes Kirkgate'. Nevertheless this detailed information enabled the commissioners to conclude that all the houses in Kirkgate, apart from one, and all living on Call Lane, from Kirkgate to Call Stile, owed suit and service to the manor and were therefore free to grind their corn where they wished. The spurious claim by the lessee of Leeds mill had, quite rightly, been dismissed; however, this was not to be the end of the matter.

The dispute was to flare up again in 1615 when Sir Arthur Ingram acquired both the manor of Leeds Kirkgate and the fee-farm of Leeds corn-mill. Ingram was infuriated by the actions of William Bainton, the miller of Hunslet, who had three horses, mares or geldings which carried thirty to forty cartloads of grain from Kirkgate to Hunslet each week and then returned it as flour. His servants regularly picked up corn from the houses of Alexander Smith, Will Adcock, Thomas Butterfield and John Watson of Kirkgate. To make matters worse, Ingram was also aware that the servants of Mary Marshall of Scott (Hall) Mill had also been seen picking up corn from his Kirkgate tenants. Despite the earlier ruling Ingram filed another action to try and force his Kirkgate tenants to grind their corn at his mill but he was no more successful than John Lyndley had been in 1599.[49] But this is taking us into the seventeenth century, and it is to this we turn in the next chapter.

The Rise of the Merchants:
Kirkgate in the Seventeenth Century

View of Leeds Bridge from Lodge's Prospect, c.1680.

As we have seen, from the middle of the sixteenth century Leeds had become an increasingly important centre of the West Riding woollen cloth industry; it became a town full of clothiers. The distinct feature of the seventeenth century, however, was the rise of the merchant community. As the merchant-dominated Corporation of Kingston upon Hull complained to the Crown in 1596 referring to the townspeople of Leeds: 'divers of them are not only clothiers but merchants also to the great hindrance of the merchants here and York'. Again in 1616 they complained about: 'a set of young adventurers [i.e. merchant adventurers] that are lately sprung up at Leeds and at other places amongst the clothiers, who at little or no charge buy and engross as they please to the great hurt of the inhabitants and merchants of this town'.

This increasingly wealthy group of dynamic Leeds merchants, some of whom had risen from the ranks of the town's clothiers and others who were incomers, was determined to promote the prosperity of Leeds and their business interests by gaining control of the town and its industry. Already in 1588 they had purchased the advowson of the parish church (giving them the right to choose the future vicars of Leeds).

In 1620 they took control of the town's charities by having them vested in the wonderfully-named 'Committee of Pious Uses'. Most crucially of all, in 1626 they successfully petitioned the king to incorporate the town. The royal charter granted by Charles I created the Leeds Corporation which gave them substantial powers of regulation of the manufacture of woollen cloth in the newly-created municipal borough of Leeds which had the same boundaries as the parish. Finally in 1629 a group of them bought the manor of Leeds for the princely sum of £2,710 from the Corporation of London, which had acquired it from the king in settlement of some of his debts. The merchant community was now in the driving seat.

Unfortunately few records relating to the manor of Kirkgate and its affairs survive from the confiscation of Holy Trinity's lands by the Crown in the year 1538 to the seventeenth century. This changes in 1610 when Sir Arthur Ingram purchased the manor together with the former Holy Trinity lands at Holbeck. Ingram had made a fortune dealing in property, including the sale of royal lands.[50] His purchase of Temple Newsam in June 1622 gave him the opportunity to establish a new and lasting aristocratic dynasty.[51] He also acquired the lease of the ancient mill on the River Aire, built a new corn-mill with a fulling facility adjoining it and held the bailiwick of the manor of Leeds with the common oven. In this way he became a powerful figure in the life of both Kirkgate and the town as a whole.

Sir Arthur Ingram (c.1565-1642). Portrait by George Geldorp. (Leeds Museums and Galleries)

Close up of the Manor House taken from a 1909 photograph. It was the 17th century home to the Fairfaxs, Watkinsons and Lowthers. (Leeds Library and Information Services)

Though Sir John Savile and the wealthy benefactor cloth merchant John Harrison (in practice the first alderman or mayor of Leeds) are today most remembered as the leading actors in securing the merchants' control of Leeds in the first forty years of the seventeenth century, of equal importance was Richard Sykes, the wealthy merchant who negotiated the purchase of the manor of Leeds when he was alderman in 1629. Though he lived on Briggate, his father and grandfather had both been Kirkgate clothiers.

The survey associated with the purchase of the manor confirms the great expansion that had taken place in the manufacture of cloth in Leeds. It records the proliferation of fulling mills within the manor: there were now nine plus a specialist mill for grinding redwood or Brazil wood which produced a red dye used by the clothiers.[52]

Sykes and his fellow merchants made Leeds internationally famous with their great reputation for selling cheap woollen cloth that represented excellent value for money. The nearby port of Hull gave them easy access to markets across Europe.

In the late 1620s another notable family of the period arrived in Kirkgate — the Lowthers. At the tender age of sixteen William Lowther (1612-88) was sent to Leeds by his father, a lawyer in Kendal, to be apprenticed to William Busfield (1578-1640), a successful cloth merchant in the town. Busfield, perhaps of York, had married well, securing the hand of Elizabeth, sister of Thomas Metcalfe (d.1650), one of the wealthiest Leeds merchants and holder of a one-ninth share of the manor of Leeds.[53] Lowther prospered under his master's instruction and in 1634 set up a business of his own in the town in partnership with his uncle Robert and his brother, Christopher. The following year he was admitted to the Freedom of the Fellowship of Merchant Adventurers of England which allowed him to trade with Holland, Zealand, Brabant, Flanders and Calais.

In 1636 he married Busfield's daughter, Jane (1615-86), and went to live in a house on Boar Lane, where their first two children were born. Soon after that however they moved into the most prestigious house in Kirkgate, next to the parish church, the religious and social centre of the town. It occupied the site of the old Kirkgate manor house which had been redeveloped to provide spacious, modern accommodation for people of high rank.

Recent residents had been Edward Fairfax (1568-1635?), third son of Sir Thomas Fairfax

(1521-1600) of Denton Hall, an eminent poet and author of several learned treatises, and Dr Henry Watkinson, Chancellor and Vicar General to four Archbishops of York, and so Lowther's occupancy of this property marked his rise in status within the town. This talented, fiercely ambitious man, became Sir John Lowther, a Justice of the Peace, Deputy-Lieutenant, and eventually High Sheriff of the County.[54]

Perhaps the most famous incomers of them all were the Thoresbys. Ralph Thoresby's grandfather, John, and his great uncle Paul, from West Cottingwith in North Yorkshire, settled in Leeds in the early seventeenth century as clothiers, though clearly with aspirations to be merchants. Both served as members of the corporation and joined the Leeds elite. John (1593-1661) became Alderman in 1645 and his brother Paul (d.1673) in 1660.[55] It was John who purchased the property on Kirkgate which was to become the family house where his son John (1625-1679), Ralph Thoresby's father, and Ralph, the famous Leeds historian, grew up pursuing the family's cloth merchant business.

There was already a timber-framed house dated 1508 on the plot when John the elder purchased the property. This was too small and unimposing for a wealthy cloth merchant and so he built a sizable extension and further enlarged in 1653 when a gabled extension was built to the rear.

Bust of John Thoresby (1625-1679) in Leeds Minster.

Ralph Thoresby's house on Kirkgate. This view shows the rear extensions added by Ralph's grandfather John. The house was wide comprising both the red and white gabled extensions. (PB)

Ralph Thoresby (1658-1725).
(Leeds Library and Information Services)

Traumatic Times: War and Plague

By the late 1630s and '40s Kirkgate was inhabited by both clothiers and merchants. There was a close bond between clothiers and merchants and no doubt they frequently met in the inns of the town. Fortunately for us we have a remarkably detailed description of Kirkgate's most important inn, the Golden Cock, in 1644. The inn stood close to the extremely busy junction of Kirkgate and Briggate, just to the right of where Fish Street is today; it was the ideal location to attract passing trade. In its yard it had a brew house, stables and a cock-pit where cock fighting took place. By chance the inn was described during one of the most dramatic periods in the history of Kirkgate.

The Civil War had broken out in August 1642 when Charles I had raised his standard at Nottingham. The Cavaliers and Roundheads were to contest the possession of Leeds on a number of occasions, most notably on 23 January 1643, the day of the Battle of Briggate when the Parliamentary forces of Sir Thomas Fairfax swept the Royalist troops out of Leeds. Three months later Leeds came under siege from the Royalist side, canon firing upon it from what subsequently became known as Cavalier Hill (today's Richmond Hill or The Bank). Some of the more impetuous Kirkgate residents, like John Thoresby the younger, had joined the Parliamentary cause, giving loyal service to the Fairfax family, to whom he became very close. He fought alongside them at the Battle of Marston Moor on 2 July 1644 which effectively ended with defeat for Charles I. Just eight days earlier, as a result of the death of Christopher Standeven, the landlord of the Golden Cock, an inventory of the whole inn and its contents was made. One imagines Standeven had had a very stressful time in the previous two and a half years! With large numbers of troops garrisoned in Leeds during the Civil War no doubt his inn had been overwhelmed with billeting senior officers and the custom of the soldiers, not to mention Royalist cannon balls flying nearby.

On 24 June 1644 four men were summoned to make an inventory of the contents of the inn. This fascinating document provides a real insight into the layout and contents of the building. It describes its extensive accommodation and gives the names of many of the rooms including the Cock, the Maydenhead, the Bulhead, the Murrian, the Grayhound, the Sonne, the Starr Chamber, the Throslenest, the Gloabe and the Moone. Two rooms were used for food preparation and several others clearly doubled-up as accommodation. An unusually high number of them were heated.

A drawing of the Golden Cock Inn based on a painting dated 1800 (Leeds Library and Information Services). To the rear was the brew house, a stable and a cock-pit. Cock-fighting was extremely popular in the seventeenth century and lured aristocrats and gentry into the town. Arthur Ingram, 3rd Viscount Irwin of Temple Newsam (d.1702), Lord of the Manor of Kirkgate, particularly enjoyed the sport. Fish Street is to the left of the inn.

The Golden Cock Inn Inventory

In 1613 Christopher Standeven of York married Agnes Currer in Leeds and it seems likely that it is through this marriage that he gained an interest in the Kirkgate property. He does not appear to have made a success of the venture and had failed to pay for a wine licence. The Lord Treasurer issued a warrant for collection of the debt. On 4 January 1637 Thomas Westley reported that he had journeyed to Leeds from London and secured payment of £9 for the wine licence plus his own travelling expenses.[56]

The inventory suggests that the inn was in some disarray or rundown — perhaps the effects of the war or the fact that Standeven was probably at least into his 60s by then; the contents included *'one ould stoole… 2 ould bridle byts…one old Lyne wheele…one Broken Ladder… old Tubbes and nyne old Hogsheades'*. There are no details of the valuables, no doubt friends and relatives had already removed them.

An Inventory of all such goodes as are now founde & remainyng in the dwellinge house in Ledes Kirkgate wherein mr Standeven late dwelt prised and valued the 24 day of June 1644 by 4 indefferent men.

Imprimis in [one interlined] Roome called the Cock [and in the studdy deleted] one Iron Range one draw Table two litle square Tables one forme one lyverey Cubberd two Chares 2 stooles 1 stoole frame xxviijs

Item in the study one ould covered stoole and some smale roddes and [one deleted] 2 ould brydle byts ijs iiijd

Imprimis in the Lowe roome called maydenhead one Iron Range one Cupbord & one liverey Cupbord one Square Table two Chayers one litle Table 5 stooles xlijs

Imprimis in the great kitchinge Called Bulhead one square Table And one other Table one long Iron Range 3 Chayers 3 stooles one Glass Case 2 litle Cupbordes xxxvs

Imprimis in the litle kitchinge called the Murrian one Iron Range one Cupbord and one Table xvis

Item the Roome called the Grayhound one Table one stand bed & one Trundle bed 3 Buffett stooles xxs

Item in the Chamber called the Sonne one Iron Range one Table one liverey Cupbord one litle Table fouer stooles one stand Bed & 2 Curten Rodds xxvijs

Imprimis in that Chamber called the starr Chamber one Table one Iron Rang one Chist one stand Bed one Fall bed 3 stooles one Chayer and 3 Curten Rodes xxviijs

Item in the litle Chamber called the Throslenest one Table one stock bed vs

Imprimis in that Chamber called the Gloabe one Iron Range one long Table And two short Tables one stand Bedd with 3 Iron Curten Rodes three stooles one seelinge Chayer And one Chist xlviijs

Item in the Chamber called the Moone one Iron Rang one stand Bed two Curten Rodes one natt one Table one Chist one stoole xxs
Item in the Chamber next adioyninge three Tubbes one old Lyne wheele iijs

Item in the Brewhouse [several words deleted] two Great Tubbs one Great Cooler one stone Trough one lead Carbe one Scoope one Hen Call one Broken Ladder with other huslements xls

Item in the stable & the Ostery certayne old Tubbes is

Item in the seller 5 payer of Gantrees and nyne old hogsheades & Pypes & one safe xxxs

Item on the Backside one greate stone Trough and one Brewing lead in the brewhouse are both of them unprised.

[signed by]

John Wilson   Arthur Beston marke +

Thomas Walker   Ja. Stireinge

Note: The valuations are given in Roman numerals. For example:

ijs iiijd = 2 shillings 4 pence
xxs = 20 shillings

29

No sooner had the Civil War come to an end than the residents of Kirkgate were rocked by a catastrophic visitation of the plague in 1645. The first victim in Leeds was Alice Musgrave who lived close by in Vicar Lane and was buried on 11 March. Within nine months over 1,325 Leeds people had died, over one-fifth of the parish's population. The inhabitants of Kirkgate must have been traumatised; the outbreak was particularly bad in Marsh Lane, The Calls and Lower Briggate but worst of all in Vicar Lane.

Searchers, watchmen, keepers and 'buryers' were appointed. Suspected sufferers and their households were moved to specially constructed cabins on Quarry Hill, while their homes were locked up. With so many people dying emergency burial sites were created with large numbers of the dead being buried in Vicar's Croft and North Hall orchard. The 'ould church [parish church] doors were shut up and prayers and sermon onely [held] at the New Church [St John's]'. Fortunately by Christmas the worst was over and the onset of winter killed off the sources of infection.

The Return of Prosperity and Daily Life within the Manor

It is testimony to the great dynamism and resilience of the Leeds community that the town's woollen cloth trade bounced back remarkably well in the second half of the seventeenth century from the great shocks of the Civil War and the plague. By mid-century the cloth industry began to recover and the great cloth market held on Tuesdays and Saturdays on and near Leeds Bridge began to thrive once more.

Kirkgate continued to be dominated by clothiers and clothworkers, their modest houses a hive of industry producing large quantities of cloth for both the domestic and export markets. The will and inventory of William Dixon of Kirkgate in 1663 shows the life of the Kirkgate clothiers was going on much as they had before these disasters.

The structure of their houses was still timber-framed, but they tended to be larger than those of their Tudor counterparts. They had fireplaces with chimneys instead of fire-hoods, and plaster ceilings instead of open timbers in the formal rooms. The contents of Dixon's house were certainly more sophisticated than those possessed by clothiers a century earlier. His home still contained the great range of tools necessary for the production of broadcloth but in the main room of the house were seven stools, four chairs, three tables and nine cushions. An elaborate iron cooking range with two andirons, two spits and a pair of iron racks with 'other Iron geere' dominated the room which also held a number of brass pots and a frying pan. Here too was his purse and apparel worth £21 6s. The parlour had two beds, a foot chest, a cupboard, one safe, three additional chests, one trunk, a vast range of bedding, four cushions and eleven pieces of pewter.

Fortunately, three years of records from the court books of the Lord Ingram's manor of 'Leeds Kirkgate-cum-Holbeck' survive for 1666-68. These give a wonderful insight into everyday life within the manor, with poor roads, ill maintained pavements and unyoked pigs being just a few of the dangers to avoid.[57]

On 6 October 1666 John Stanhope, steward of the owner of the manor, Viscount Irwin of Temple Newsam, visited Kirkgate to preside over the View of Frankpledge and Court Leet. According to Thoresby these courts were held in the tithe barn just to the west of the parish church. Business was brisk. Sixty two people from the manor were immediately fined for non-attendance. Robert Chipping was chosen as constable and then the accused were summoned and judged. Among the miscreants fined that day were John Walker, bricklayer, for leaving his well uncovered 'to the great danger of passers-by', Thomas Dixon, gentleman, who had failed to repair the road leading to the Church, Richard Nelson for leaving wood lying in the street and Isaac Blackburn for scouring hides at a certain place called 'Le Common Stay.'

Twelve months later the nature of the complaints had changed and it appears that violence was on the increase. Nicholas Hall, alias Bradberry, appeared before John Stanhope and the jury. He was clearly a nasty piece of work! He was fined 5s for an assault on Widow Blackburn, a pauper, 5s for 'drawing blood on the body of Robert Newam' and a further 3s 4d for allowing his un-muzzled dog to bite several people.

Samuel Burrow, Junior, had lost patience with another difficult character of the district called John Walker who owed him 5s 3d. Samuel had taken the law into his own hands and kept Walker prisoner for nearly twenty four hours! It was 'garbage' and pigs that dominated the October session of 1668. William Marshall was fined 3s 4d for casting his dunghill on the high road 'to the nuisance of passers-by' and Thomas Franch had placed his pigsty so near the water that he fouled the stream for those lower down the beck. In December 1669 Thomas Illingworth was fined 3s.4d. for allowing his swine to feed in the churchyard!

The Families of Late Seventeenth Century Kirkgate

Another wonderful survival which tells us much about Kirkgate in the late 1660s is the Hearth Tax Return. The Hearth Tax had been levied from 1662 onwards to raise money for Charles II and gives us information about the population of Kirkgate and the size of their homes. The population and the number of properties in the manor had more than quadrupled over the 123 years since the 24 properties were noted in 1545. On 14 July 1668 the Justices of the Peace commanded the local constables to assess the number of hearths in the town. Inhabitants in receipt of poor relief or living in houses worth less than twenty shillings per annum and not paying parish rates were exempt, the rest had to pay two shillings per hearth.

Altogether there were 114 households listed, 47 had a single hearth, 33 had two hearths and 16 had three.[58] Above this, 18 households occupied houses with four hearths or more. Interestingly in the case of the wealthier households a pattern emerges of the importance of the extended family with relatives living next door to each other – Alice Pawson, widow, and her son, Christopher (d.1694), had four hearths apiece; brothers James and Joseph Ibbetson had six and seven hearths respectively. John Thoresby (1625-79) and his brother Timothy (d.1670) both had five hearths. Bridget Allanson had seven hearths and her daughter-in-law, Mary Allanson, next door, had nine.

It is fascinating to see in this document familiar names that demonstrate the longevity of families' residence in Kirkgate, most notably the Pawsons. The Allansons too were a very significant family. Bridget's husband, the wealthy merchant Francis Allanson who had died six years earlier, had been Alderman of Leeds in 1644 and 1657. He had been a staunch supporter of Parliament, and had made a fortune between the Civil War and the restoration of Charles II to the throne in 1660 from the cloth trade and as a sequestrator of Royalist property. Bridget continued after her husband's death to be involved in money-lending and pawnbroking.[59]

The Thoresbys too are by now familiar from earlier pages but a name new to us is Ibbetson, a family whose members will figure prominently in the later story of Kirkgate. Although a tradition of intermarriage between the families of the established merchant and professional classes forming Leeds Corporation created the impression of a stable and closed Leeds elite, in fact newcomers to the town could quite quickly find their way into the heart of its ranks. The Ibbetson family did so around the 1660s. The family had lived in Leeds since the late sixteenth century but had prospered in the Interregnum, becoming members of the inner élite. Like the Pawson family they had ceased to be clothiers and instead became regarded as 'merchants'. When James Ibbetson died in 1672, he left significant property and a share in a Hull ship to his children.[60]

Pawson's two-bayed and Cookson's five-bayed timber-framed houses on Kirkgate.
(Leeds Library and Information Services)

Another highly important family of incomers which was to rise high in the merchant community and become prominent in the story of Kirkgate were the Cooksons; though they just missed inclusion in the Hearth Tax returns. The family came from long established yeoman farmers in the Settle area. Around 1652 William Cookson (1639-1716), the second son of Brian Cookson (c.1610-1685), travelled to Leeds to seek his fortune in the burgeoning cloth trade.[61] He prospered and fifteen years later married Hannah Greathead. He leased an estate near the parish church which included a sizeable timber-framed house abutting Kirkgate where on 17 October 1669 Hannah gave birth to the first of eight children. Two weeks later the couple walked the short distance to the parish church where the child was baptised William, after his father.[62] In 1685 William senior was elected a member of Leeds Corporation and signed the Declaration of Loyalty to Charles II. In 1697 he purchased the estate in Kirkgate and expanded the house to make decent accommodation for his growing family.

We are extremely fortunate that among the surviving papers of Ralph Thoresby, there is another document which, in the days long before censuses were taken, tells us much about the residents of Kirkgate in the 1690s. It is 'An Assessment made this 5 July 1692….by a certain Act of Parliament… for carrying on a Vigourous Warr against France'.[63]

Ralph Thoresby and Samuel Ibbetson, as trusted local worthies, had been required to visit every house in the manor of 'Leeds Kirkgate' to assess how much tax each household was liable to pay. Once the assessment was made the money was collected by fellow residents Christopher Conder and Samuel Atkinson. The document essentially provides us with a census of residents and their relative wealth. This enables us to understand the social and economic composition of the residents of Kirkgate and The Calls. Assuming that no destitute or very poor households were excluded from the assessment, there were 96 houses with 292 occupants, 110 adult males, 114 adult females and 68 children. A further two houses had recently become unoccupied.

At a time when a journeyman weaver or clothworker perhaps earned around 3 to 4 shillings a week at this time (it would not be higher), the minimum payment of 1 shilling which 23 households paid would be much resented, as would the 2 to 3 shillings paid by another 40 better off households. But at the top of the scale the 13 to 27 shillings paid by the 17 wealthiest residents would not have seemed like a king's ransom. The rich and the poor really did live cheek by jowl with the gap in incomes and assets writ large — two-thirds of the Kirkgate households paid 3 shillings or less, while one-sixth paid at least four times as much. In this lowest two-thirds, only two households had servants: theirs were perhaps unusual circumstances — Matthew Wroe's widow had no doubt fallen on hard times but retained the family servant; Thomas Johnson had an apprentice and a maid, perhaps he was a widowed craftsman or clothier. Of the six households assessed in the higher bracket of 4 shillings we find three men with family and an apprentice. Almost every one of the 22 households assessed at 7 shillings or above included 2 to 4 children (41 of the 68 noted in the assessment) and a maid; 4 of the 7 wealthiest households had 2 maids.

One looks for specific evidence of the clothiers and merchants. The occupations of most heads of households are not given but we see that four households in the 3 to 8 shilling bracket had an apprentice. No household was assessed at 9 to 12 shillings, so it is in 17 households in the 13 shilling or above bracket that we see the merchant and larger clothier class emerge, there were 9 people designated as 'Tradesman' (Thoresby's term for a clothier) and only 2 as 'Marchant'. No doubt these 'tradesmen' clothiers' activities were more concerned with the purchase and co-ordination of the manufacture of cloth rather than organising its export in ships to foreign parts and therefore Thoresby reserved the title of 'marchant' for the high status gentlemanly foreign export merchants. Ralph Thoresby assessed at 14 shillings with his wife, child and maid did not give his own occupation but at the top of the tree we find at 18 shillings Mr John Dodshon, Tradesman, 4 children, 1 maid, one apprentice; at 19 shillings Mr William Cookson, Tradesman, wife, 4 children, 2 maids, 1 apprentice, and Mr William Cotton, Tradesman, 4 children, 2 maids, 2 apprentices; at 21 shillings Alderman Joshua Ibbetson, Commissioner; at 23 shillings Mr Henry Pawson, Marchant, wife & maid; at 24 shillings Mr Killingbeck, Vicar, wife and 2 maids, and Mr John Spink, Attorney, wife, child & maid; and at the very top at 27 shillings Mr Samuel Ibbetson, Marchant, wife, 3 children and 2 maids.

Bakehouses Old and New

lawyer, held two-ninths of the manor and were entitled to that percentage of the profit. Secondly, a number of people operated their own ovens. The situation was chaotic! The corporation appointed Thomas Dixon and William Hutchinson, two of the Aldermen, and William Fenton, James Netherwood, Robert Nesse and Samuel Sykes, four of the Common Council, to advise as to whether the oven should be rebuilt and, if not, how to introduce a scheme to licence bakers' ovens. Over twelve years later they were still trying to find a solution to the problem.[68]

The difficulties of imposing law and order during the Civil War provided ambitious and opportunistic bakers with a chance to construct their own ovens, like the one above. It proved impossible to apply the manorial monopoly of baking, yet these ancient medieval rights were still held by the Crown and had been passed directly to Leeds Corporation in return for an annual rent.[64]

By 1662 the bakehouse was in a ruinous state. Edward Atkinson, the deputy mayor, and two aldermen were empowered to try and sell the premises. On 8 November Atkinson reported that William Milner, one of the richest merchants in the town, had offered to buy them for £60.[65] For some reason the sale did not go ahead and seven years later scant progress had been made.[66]

By 1669 'many and vast buildings Lately erected and Adjoining became very dangerous for dreade of any Suddann and accidentall fire'.[67] The recent fire of London had highlighted the dangers associated with bakehouses and the location and condition of the Leeds oven made it a genuine hazard. The corporation proposed that it should be rebuilt in order to raise money to pay rent to the king but there were complications. Firstly, it did not hold all the rights of the lord of the manor relating to the oven which had been purchased in 1629: Ralph Thoresby and Richard Wilson, a

The corporation finally decided to purchase the outstanding manorial rights so that it could once and for all eradicate this potential burden on the people of Leeds.[69] On 14 November 1709 Ralph Thoresby and Richard Wilson, who had both inherited their shares in the manor from their fathers-in-law, sold their rights to the corporation for £160. The corporation was now free to sell the site to the Ibbetson family who then developed 'The Square'.[70]

Peter Brears' reconstruction drawing above is of a seventeenth-century bakehouse which was discovered by workmen around 1880 in the front cellar of no. 8 Kirkgate (on the north side of the street just to the west of Fish Street). The building had been purchased by Ward & Co, wholesale provision and egg merchants, who already occupied no. 9 and were building an extension to their shop on the site of no. 8. It had an eighteen foot frontage on Kirkgate and its cellar was nine feet deep. Details of the find are included in the contemporary notes of John Holmes, a Victorian antiquary, held in a private collection.

The Merchants' Golden Age:
Kirkgate in the Eighteenth Century

The Prospect of Leeds From the Knostrop Road, 1715 by Francis Place. (Ducatus Leodiensis)

Leeds Cloth Market and the First White Cloth Hall

Kirkgate in the eighteenth century was dominated by its merchant families and the cloth industry. Before taking a detailed tour of the locality in the early 1720s as if with its most famous resident Ralph Thoresby, let us begin with the story of its most important building, the First White Cloth Hall – undoubtedly the most significant historic building still standing in Leeds today, though in a ruinous condition.

Though unworldly and obsessed with his antiquarian pursuits, Thoresby played a pivotal role in ensuring that Leeds stayed ahead of its close rival, Wakefield, in the sale of white and coloured cloth. For centuries Leeds cloth market had been located on Leeds Bridge and then extended up Briggate. Clothiers from the surrounding area brought their cloth there for sale to the Leeds merchants, who had it finished and then exported to the continent or to other parts of Britain.

Right until the end of the eighteenth century cloth making was essentially a handicraft industry. Furthest west in the woollen cloth area the clothiers worked in isolated farmhouses but as you got closer to Leeds increasingly they were located in villages such as Beeston, Armley, Holbeck, Hunslet, and Morley. The towns of Wakefield, Huddersfield, Halifax and Bradford but, above all Leeds, became dominated by cloth finishing and cloth marketing, and supplied the foodstuffs and everyday needs of the clothiers in their hinterland.[71]

By 1700 Leeds was by far the largest and most important market centre for the woollen cloth-producing area. At that time one-fifth of the woollen cloth produced in England was made in the West Riding.

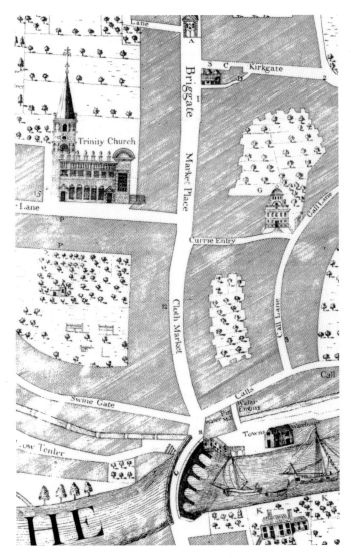

The Briggate Cloth Market on Cossins' Plan, 1726.

The Briggate Cloth Market. (PB)

The Leeds cloth market in Briggate was pronounced one of the wonders of the world.[72] In the 1720s Daniel Defoe wrote a marvellous description of it:

> Early in the morning, there are trestles placed in two rows in the street, sometimes two rows on a side.......... then there are boards laid across those trestles, so that the boards lie like long counters on either side, from one end of the street to the other. The clothiers come early in the morning with their cloth; and as few clothiers bring more than one piece, the market being so frequent, they go into the inns and public-houses with it, and there set it down.

> At seven o' clock in the morning,.......... the market bell rings; it would surprise a stranger to see in how few minutes, without hurry or noise, and not the least disorder, the whole market is filled; all the boards upon the trestles are covered with cloth, close to one another as the pieces can lie long ways by one another, and behind the piece of cloth, the clothier standing to sell it..........

> .... As soon as the bell has done ringing, the merchants and factors, and buyers of all sorts, come down, and coming along the spaces between the row of boards, they walk up the rows, and down as their occasion direct. Some of them have their foreign letters of orders, with patterns sealed on them, in rows, in their hands; and with those they match colours, holding them to the cloths as they think they agree to; when they see any cloths to their colours, or that suit their occasions, they reach over to the clothier and whisper, and in the fewest words imaginable the price is stated; one asks, the other bids; and 'tis agree, or not agree, in a moment.......... Thus, you see, ten or twenty thousand pounds value in cloth, and sometimes much more, bought and sold in little more than an hour, and the laws of the market the most strictly observed as ever I saw done in any market in England.[73]

Having bought the cloth, the merchants had the cloth finished and then exported it to the continent or to other parts of Britain.

Clothiers carrying their cloth by pack horse to Leeds Market. (George Walker, The Costume of Yorkshire, 1814)

The Port of Leeds. This illustration by Peter Brears, based on an engraving of 1801, looks upstream to the medieval Leeds Bridge. Warehouse Hill and the Aire and Calder Navigation wharf and 'Town Warehouse' are on the right. The engraving, at the top of a list of local woolstaplers (middlemen dealing in wool), was dedicated to Samuel Birchall.

At this time river transport was the cheapest and most efficient way to move goods and so the port facilities had been expanded and improved to cope with the growing demand for locally produced cloth. The opening of the Aire and Calder navigation in 1701 transformed the speed with which goods could reach the sea-going ships based at Hull. At the beginning of the eighteenth century Holland and Germany had been the most important markets for cloth but one of the features of the century was the success of Leeds merchants in expanding the market to include Spain, Portugal, Italy and North America.

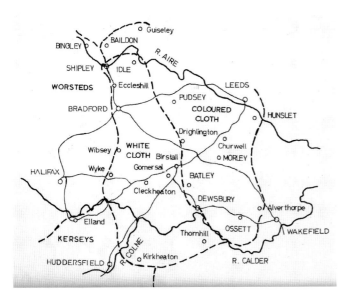

Plan of the cloth producing areas of the West Riding.

The woollen cloth brought to Leeds market was of two types: coloured cloth and white cloth. Coloured cloth was made with wool which the clothiers had already dyed whilst white cloth was made with undyed wool. Clothiers specialised in making one type. Coloured cloth was made in Leeds and its neighbouring villages; whereas white cloth was made much further away, in an arc running from Bradford to Wakefield. Despite the fact that Leeds was far to the north-east of the white cloth producing area, it was the principal market centre for white cloth; indeed Morley was the closest village that made this type of fabric. This was to cause trouble!

The area specialising in coloured or mixed cloth included Leeds parish, Morley, Gildersome, Pudsey, Farsley, Idle, Yeadon, Guiseley and Horsforth — chiefly the Aire Valley plus Batley, Ossett, Horbury and Calder Valley. Meanwhile the white cloth area included Alverthorpe, Ossett, Kirkheaton, Dewsbury, Batley, Mirfield, Cleckheaton, Littleton, Bowling, Shipley, Morley, Idle and villages around Bradford. The first major challenge to the commercial supremacy of Leeds came in 1709 when the lords of the manor of Hightown, a mere hamlet near Liversedge, situated in the very heart of the white cloth area, applied to Queen Anne for a charter to hold a cloth market there. The Leeds merchants had a real fright and successfully petitioned against the granting of the charter.[74]

In 1710 Wakefield merchants too challenged the Leeds merchants' dominance in the white cloth trade by erecting a covered market hall for the sale of white cloth. The cloths made around Wakefield were generally broad white cloths, a type for which Leeds thought it alone had the market. For many clothiers the Wakefield cloth hall was closer than Leeds and, of course, more comfortable than the open air Briggate street market, especially in winter.

If Wakefield had been allowed to excel Leeds in its facilities, it might soon have detached a large number of white cloth manufacturers who were then coming to Leeds from places in the Calder Valley. In 1700 Wakefield was second to Leeds in the marketing of cloth and was significantly smaller; Leeds having a population of around 6,000 compared to its rival's 3,500. Water transport was critically important to the commercial success and growth of towns in the eighteenth century, and Leeds and Wakefield cloth merchants had teamed up to make the Rivers Aire and Calder navigable to where the Aire joined the River Ouse, giving them access to the port of Hull. When the Aire and Calder Navigation opened in 1700, Wakefield became a real threat to Leeds' commercial success. In 1710 when Wakefield opened its cloth hall, the Leeds merchants responded immediately!

Ralph Thoresby noted in his diary on 12 August 1710: 'With the Corporation ....consulting upon erecting a hall for the white cloths.' Two days later he wrote:

> Rode with [the] Mayor, cousin Milner, and others to my Lord Irwin [at Temple Newsam], about the erection of a hall for the white cloths in Kirkgate, to prevent the damage to this town by one lately erected at Wakefield, with design to engross [the woollen cloth trade] which is computed to bring above one hundred tradesmen [clothiers] every market-day to this town, which [it] would utterly prevent for the future if permitted[75].

Edward Machell, Lord Ingram, 4th Viscount Irwin (1686-1714). (Leeds Museums and Galleries)

Money for the Leeds White Cloth Hall was speedily raised from merchants and clothiers in the town. The capital was raised in thirty-two shares at £24 10s each, making a total of £784, which accords with Thoresby's statement that it cost near £1000.

In his great work on Leeds, *Ducatus Leodiensis*, Ralph proudly describes the hall which opened in 1711:

> A stately Hall for White Cloths erected at near a Thousand Pounds Charge by certain Merchants and Tradesmen in Town; 'tis built upon Pillars and Arches in the Form of an Exchange, with a Quadrangular Court within: Both the higher and lower stories are replenished with the Sort of Goods; which till this Juncture, the Makers had to carry Samples of to each of the Merchants Houses they dealt with; and these had the Trouble, upon emergent Occasions, to ride to the several Townships or Hamlets of Heaton, Berkenshaw, and Bradford-dale, Alverthorpe, Birstall, Little-town, Mirfield, Clifton and Hathet, as they are enumerated upon the Doors of the distinct Repositories, where the Goods are lodged till the weekly Markets upon Tuesdays Afternoon, of which Notice is given by the Bell in a beautiful Cupulo painted and gilt.[76]

Irwin, then aged 24, was lord of the manor of Kirkgate and owned the site occupied by the derelict hospitium and former chantry priest's house on which the merchants proposed to build the new hall. Happily they received a positive response and in Thoresby's words, Irwin 'gave all the encouragement imaginable'.

Trading in the hall took place in the afternoon on Tuesdays, so merchants could go there after attending the cloth market in Briggate in the morning. The white cloth being sold here was not the sort normally sold in the Briggate cloth market. This suggests that the clothiers (Thoresby refers to them as 'tradesmen') using the hall were of the larger sort, who were producing and selling cloth in larger quantities than the typical clothier, and each had several journeymen weavers and spinners working for them. The fact that merchants previously would ride over to the townships to buy the cloth if they needed it at short notice, suggests that it was of a higher quantity than the norm. Thanks to this hall, and to the great expansion in trade during the eighteenth century, the market for white cloths flourished in Leeds over the next forty years. As we shall see later the First White Cloth Hall also fulfilled an important social function for the rapidly improving town by providing excellent new accommodation for dances, concerts and gambling. The first assembly was held in the cloth hall on 11 June 1712.

First White Cloth Hall on Cossins' Plan.

First White Cloth Hall, Kirkgate elevation. A conjectural view based on the available evidence. (PB)

First White Cloth Hall, rear elevation. (PB)

The First White Cloth Hall in Use and its Later History

White Cloth Hall today

On the south side of Kirkgate are the remains of the First White Cloth Hall, a remarkable building that has stayed in use for over three centuries.

The Moot Hall, Briggate (Joseph Rhodes 1825).
(Leeds Museums and Galleries)

Its architect was almost certainly William Etty of York. Its construction began in 1710, the same year the Corporation had commissioned Etty to rebuild the Moot Hall on Briggate. Indeed, Thoresby, on the very day he was consulting with the Corporation upon erecting a hall for the white cloths, noted that 'the foundation of the front of the new Guildhall was now laid, the engines exercised, etc'.

What better person could they turn to than Etty who had also designed the Thursday Market Cross in York, erected six years earlier? The similarities between these three buildings are striking.

Thursday Market Cross in York.

Lord Irwin provided the site by allowing the demolition of the old cottages that had formed the medieval hospitium. So expeditiously was the project carried forward that only eight months after his urgent visit to Temple Newsam, Thoresby was able to write in his diary on 22 May 1711: 'went to see the New White Cloth Market in Kirkgate opened this day'.[77]

Thanks to this hall, and to the general expansion of trade during the eighteenth century, the market for white cloths flourished over the next forty years. At first the new rival Wakefield cloth hall prospered, but as time went on the competition from Leeds was too great and merchants and clothiers chiefly attended Leeds cloth market.

At the start cloth was sold in the open arcades on the ground floor and in three large rooms upstairs — the principal long room across the back and the two wings, while unsold cloth was stored until the next market day in the rooms or repositories in the cellars. The caption to Samuel and Nathaniel Buck's 1745 Prospect of Leeds noted that:

> The [Briggate] market is allow'd to be the largest in England for Broad Cloths, which are exported from hence to Germany, Italy, Spain, Portugal, and even to the most remote places of the known World. There is besides the Market for mixt Cloth already mention'd, a very handsome well built Hall for White Cloth; under which are very Convenient Cells, where the Clothiers may deposit the cloth remaining unsold from one market day to another.

At some time after the hall's erection (we do not know how long but perhaps not very long), it was apparently decided that exposure to the wind and the cold was undesirable and the ground floor arches were filled in.

The Assembly Rooms

The First White Cloth Hall was also used as an assembly room. In the first quarter of the eighteenth century the wealthy merchants of Leeds sought to live in an increasingly elegant and genteel style. For any man or woman of rank hoping to find an eligible partner in life, taking part in balls and assemblies was important. Unlike the county towns, at the start of the eighteenth century Leeds had no purpose-built assembly rooms, although the large rooms of the town's major inns might to some extent fulfil this role. The main upstairs room running across the back of the First White Cloth Hall, being 60 feet by 20 feet, made an ideal ballroom, and on such occasions, the other upstairs wings were probably used as card and supper rooms.[78]

Most certainly the sons of the gentlemen merchants of Leeds attended the assemblies to cast an eye over the eligible young ladies of the day, and vice versa. One, who named himself 'Amiator', was clearly so smitten by a Miss D-w-n that he was moved to publish an ode to her in a Leeds newspaper:[79]

To Miss D-w-n, on her Dancing at the Assembly at Leeds, April 26 1739

With what a grace Sweet Celia moves
How noble is her Mien,
Whilst ev'ry Action plainly proves
She's born o'er hearts to Reign;

My Ravish'd Eyes with Pleasure view,
Each motion as she turns,
And fatal (tho' it is) pursue
The Maze in which she runs;

Her shape, her Air, Nay! Ev'ry part
Speaks her to be divine
To so much Merit I my Heart
Can willingly resign.

Know then dear Celia that my Bliss,
So much depends on thine.
That 'tis the utmost of my wish
Thou'd be for ever mine.

   Amiator

There was a vast growth in woollen cloth production in the West Riding during the eighteenth century. In 1700 the West Riding produced 20% of woollen cloth in England, a century later that figure had risen to 60%. The success of Leeds as a great cloth marketing centre was fundamental to the prosperity of England, and it would not have achieved it without the building of the First White Cloth Hall.

Such was the expansion of the production of white cloth and the market for it that in 1755 it was decided that a bigger cloth hall was needed. A new building was erected on a strip of land between Hunslet Lane and Meadow Lane, just 220 yards south of Leeds Bridge. This opened three years later. In 1755-58 the Coloured Cloth Hall was also built with 1,770 stalls for clothiers. It was huge, running down the side of today's Infirmary Street into the heart of today's City Square where the Black Prince stands. Thus the building of the First White Cloth Hall had set in train the building of a series of cloth halls which underpinned the supremacy and huge growth of Leeds as the country's premier cloth marketing and merchanting centre.

Once the First White Cloth Hall ceased to be used for the selling of cloth it was adapted and subdivided for a variety of uses, though the long room at the back retained its use as an assembly room. It was well-used, balls and assemblies there being regularly noted in the newspapers.[80] But it too was superseded as the town's principal assembly room in 1777 when the merchants built the splendid and much larger Assembly Rooms above the north range of the new Third White Cloth Hall just behind it in The Calls.

In 1777 a market for worsted cloths was opened in the west wing of the First White Cloth Hall.[81] In 1779 part of the building was used as a Baptist Chapel and ten years later the Rev. C. Vincent opened a school in the Old Card Assembly Room for 'the for the Instruction of Youth in the English Language, Writing and Arithmetic'.[82] Nevertheless the main room at the back, by this time being known as 'The Old Assembly Room', continued to be used for enjoyable and apparently quite lavish events:

> Just arrived in Leeds, on their way to London from Edinburgh and Newcastle, who intend performing in the Old Assembly Room in Kirkgate for one week only:- This present evening will be performd by the Famous Italian Patagonian Performers, a new Comedy call'd Circe and Atlas, The Rival Magicians. Exhibiting a beautiful Transformation of a Shepherdess into a Flower Pot, then into a Fountain. Harlequin is transformed into an Ass — Diana descends from Heaven to the Assistance of Harlequin and Clora in the Great Illuminated Temple.[83]

Yet by 1800 such lavish entertainment had ceased and the sub-divided building had a multiplicity of uses; the halcyon days of bustling cloth market and elegant function rooms were long passed. The building's former importance became lost in time.

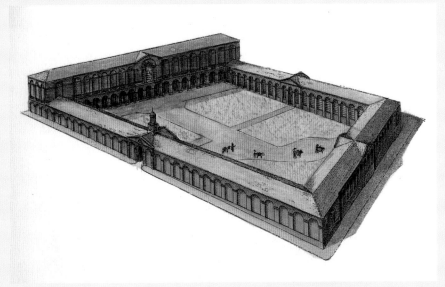

The Third White Cloth Hall opened 1776, with the 1777 Assembly Rooms above its north range. (PB)

A Tour of Kirkgate and The Calls in the early 1720s

Kirkgate shown on Samuel Buck's 'East Prospect of the Town of Leedes from Chaveler [Cavalier] Hill', 1720. (The Thoresby Society) Whilst Buck's Prospect employs considerable artistic license in both its perspective and the accuracy of the portrayal of Kirkgate's buildings, it nevertheless provides a fascinating impression of Kirkgate and its setting. No doubt the engraver struggled at times to interpret the precise detail of the artist's drawings from which he produced the printing plate. Important buildings are numbered: 8. The Old Church of St Peter's; 9. William Cookson, Esq. (presumably referring to the location of his house which is obscured by the church); 10. John Atkinson, Esq. (the dome of his house is unmistakeable); 11. The Independent Meeting House (Call Lane); 12. The White Cloth Hall (its cupola can be seen with a flag fluttering at the top, just as in the sketch on Cossins' Plan); 13. The Vicarage (just the side can be seen); 14. The Museum of Ralph Thoresby, Esq. (unlike the Vicarage, no architectural detail seems to be indicated, just the location).

When Ralph Thoresby published his ground-breaking and monumental book *Ducatus Leodiensis* (the Dukedom of Leeds) in 1715, his purpose was not to present a history of Leeds. Rather it was to take his readers on a topographical tour of his home town and its environs. As he guided them through its streets and fields he introduced information of interest about the people, past and present, the historical events, and the physical changes associated with the areas and features which he described.

Thoresby was also keen that its changing townscape and character should be recorded for posterity in prospects and panoramas which attractively and informatively pervade the pages of this book. Around 1684 he encouraged his friend William Lodge to draw the *Prospect of Leeds* which was later to adorn the pages of *Ducatus.* In 1712 he walked with Francis Place to Cavalier Hill (Richmond Hill as we know it today) to advise on the *Prospect of Leeds from Knostrop Road* which he commissioned to appear across two pages of the great work. His enthusiasm for helping to record the changes to the town never diminished.

In October 1719 and April 1720, five years after the publication of the *Ducatus*, he went to

Cavalier Hill yet again, this time with the artist Samuel Buck, to choose 'a convenient station to take a long prospect of Leeds, designed to be printed'. He returned a final time on 5 September 1720, this time with his cousin, William Cookson, to see Buck 'giving the finishing stroke to the Prospect of Leeds from Cavalier Hill'.[84]

It is to our great good fortune that just as Thoresby's life was coming to an end in 1725, the young surveyor John Cossins was contemplating the production of his town plan of Leeds.

Cossins' remarkable *New & Exact Plan of the Town of Leedes*, published in 1726, combined with the town prospects and the *Ducatus* enable your authors to lead you on a tour of Kirkgate and The Calls (the footprint of the ancient manor of Leeds Kirkgate) as if we had Thoresby at our side.

In *Ducatus* Thoresby divides his topographical tour of the town into three parts – beginning with the manorial borough based on Briggate before moving to the ancient manor of Leeds Kirkgate and finally 'Leeds Main Riding' - the surrounding land within the bounds of the manor of Leeds. Starting at the site of 'Leeds Castle' and the park, he progresses down Boar Lane, and then turns into Briggate, which he describes in great detail, before proceeding up to the Upper and Lower Head-Rows, and along 'New Street' to St John's Church and 'Town End'. He then returns to the main town, via Vicar Lane, and Kirkgate End where our tour now begins.

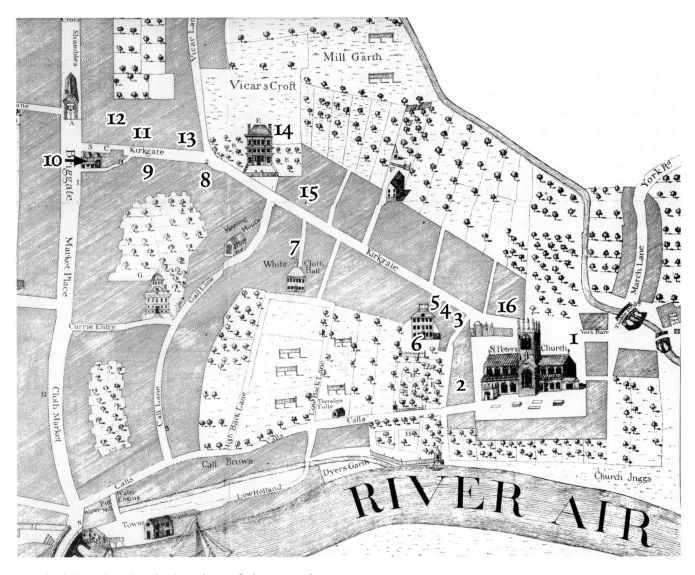

Cossins' Plan showing the locations of places on the tour.

1 Leeds Parish Church

2 Tithe Barn

3 Manor house of Kirkgate

4 Pawson's house

5 Cookson's house

6 Cookson's new mansion

7 First White Cloth Hall (site of the medieval hospitium)

8 Ibbetson's house

9 Infirmary

10 Original site of the manorial oven?

11 Golden Cock Inn

12 Site of the combined manorial oven and court house, later 'The Square'

13 Thoresby's house and museum

14 The Vicarage

15 William Denison's house

16 Barstow's mansion

Kirkgate End was the bustling, narrow and congested point where Briggate and Kirkgate met. John Cossins' Plan depicts Mr Francis Milner's twin-gabled, medieval jettied public house, with its elaborate timberwork and its alleyway running through from Briggate to Kirkgate, and a large archway leading to a courtyard and stables behind. In *Ducatus* Thoresby tells us that at the upper end of Kirkgate on the south side was the prison 'that necessary evil in a populous town'. It contained 'five or six dark and miserable apartments, without so much as a sewer or fireplace in the whole prison' and jutted out inconveniently half blocking the street.[85]

Walking a short way down the opposite side of the street, and turning up a narrow alley (today known as Fish Street) we would have arrived at the former site of the common bakehouse and its yard. The Hall of Pleas with the oven beneath had been demolished in the seventeenth century and the property now formed part of the estate of James Ibbetson (1674-1739). He had called his new development 'The Square' and had recently built 'Sundry Coach Houses and Stabling for Ten Horses' to accommodate his growing number of horses and carriages. With excellent access from Kirkgate and Vicar Lane this was the perfect location as it was within easy walking distance of his magnificent house. Thoresby, the usually mild-mannered historian, clearly loathed the man 'so grand in his coach' and his cunning ways.[86]

Returning to Kirkgate we go left, past the Golden Cock, and a little before the junction with Vicar Lane we arrive at Ralph Thoresby's house.

It now looked very different to how it had appeared in his grandfather's time. In 1678, just before his father's death, Ralph had supervised the building of a great brick chimney to protect against the risk of his home catching fire. For the same reason in 1708 he had had the front of his timber-framed house encased in brick. 'This summer', he wrote, 'I cased the house with brick, not for ornament but use; being built by my grandfather Alderman Thoresby and beautified by my dear father, it now stood in great need of repair, especially the best chamber which I had then made my library. While the forepart of the house was down, I made use of the back rooms for devotion, and generally arose before five to dispatch the family before the workmen came'.[87] It was at this point that the house lost the prominent front timber jetties that it once would have had.

Thoresby's House, Kirkgate elevation (composite image from a Victorian lantern slide and an early Victorian watercolour).

Part of Thoresby's house: a watercolour of c.1850. The double-fronted, red brick, two-storey building is the right hand part of the house. It is market 'T' on the plan overleaf. (Thoresby Society)

Thoresby's Drawing Room on the first floor of the house above, drawn by W. A. Hobson 1878. (Thoresby Society)

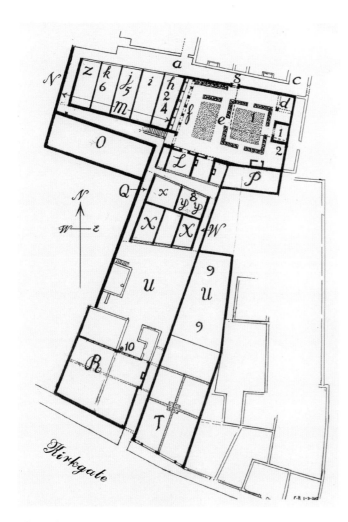

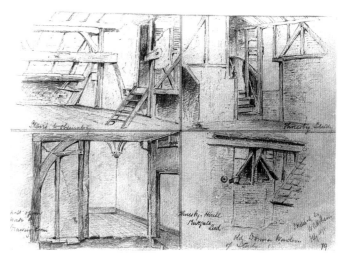

Thoresby's House interior features drawn by W. A. Hobson, shortly before its demolition in 1878. (Thoresby Society)

*Plan of Thoresby's Kirkgate property drawn c. 1724 or just after his death. Principal features from its key: **R** and **T**: John Thoresby the Elder's dwelling house; **U**: yard belonging to John Thoresby the Elder; **X**: now in the possession of Wm Lindley and Mrs Crabtree; **x**: the back kitchen; **y**: little houses; **Q**: the dark entry; **W**: the wide entry; **L**: a barn or laithe; **1**: Mr Bickerdyke's Tower; **e**: The Garden; **f**: The Piazza; **2** & **4**: late Chapman's house; **O**: museum over Mrs Howgate's premises; **a**: Piper Alley; **s**: Garden door into Piper Alley.*

Ralph was proud of some of the elegancies which the house possessed notably the stylish drawing room, perhaps once housing his library, with its groined plaster ceiling and fireplace with fine Dutch tiles. Walking down the passageway into the yard we would have encountered the drawing well in front of the detached kitchen and stable block. Ralph was pleased to have the advantage of the well but even happier when he had running water installed. In 1694 the engineer George Sorocold had constructed a water-pumping engine just below Leeds Bridge which pumped river water up to a reservoir by St John's Church from which the water was piped to the houses of the more affluent. Ralph noted excitedly in his diary on 1 October of that year: 'Was several times with Mr Sorocold's workmen who this day first began in Kirkgate to lay the lead pipes to convey water to each family.' On 7 December he obtained a full

supply when a branch from the main pipe was fixed into his kitchen.[88]

If we walked right to the bottom of Thoresby's property we would have reached the stream that flowed there (a ready supply of water was a big advantage for a merchant or clothier) and the gate in his boundary wall which conveniently gave him access into Piper Alley and within a few steps to the right into Vicar Lane. But having passed through the alley at the side of his kitchen and stable block and before reaching that gate we would have arrived at a great surprise and, for Thoresby, the great joy of his home — his ornamental garden and library and museum which, contrary to historians' long held belief, ran across the bottom of his plot. A remarkable survival is the sketch Samuel Buck made of the museum and garden when visiting Thoresby on 16 October 1719 (see picture opposite).

Ralph's father John, though a busy and successful cloth merchant, had had a very strong interest in coin collecting and antiquarian pursuits. As we have seen, he fought with distinction for the Parliamentarian side in the Civil War becoming a great friend of the celebrated commander Lord Thomas Fairfax. It was from the Fairfaxes in 1676 that he purchased an extensive collection of valuable rare coins and medals, and portraits of '150 heads of soldiers'. John's enthusiasms engendered in his son an absolute passion for all things ancient and curious; antiquarian pursuits came to dominate Ralph's life.

In addition to the coins, medals and portraits (primarily engravings), Ralph accumulated a vast collection of early manuscripts, statues, geological specimens, natural history material including eggs, shells, insects and plants and, rather ghoulishly, a series of 'human rarities' including the actual hand

Samuel Buck's Sketch of Thoresby's Museum, 1719. (Redrawn by PB)

and arm of the celebrated Marquis of Montrose. By the time of his death the collection included over 2,500 precious coins and exceptional items associated with renowned people; for example, the gold ring of Richard, Duke of York, Queen Elizabeth I's walking stick, the gloves of James I, a handkerchief of Charles I, a piece of William III's last coat, Sir Walter Raleigh's tobacco-box, and a truncheon off Sir Francis Drake's ship.

Items came from every corner of the known world, ranging from a fragment of an Egyptian mummy to a tomahawk from North Carolina; an Indian poisoned dagger and a Turkish scimitar. This immense collection was housed in the purpose-built accommodation shown in Buck's sketch. The library and museum were in the gabled, brick building to the left which was supported on an arched colonnade. One of the magnificent Gothic niches from the shrine of St William at York Minster crowned the library door while a whale's rib and scapula can be seen near the entrance to the building. We know little about the internal arrangements of the museum but the valuable coins and medals were stored in 'Boards with Cells for Coins' housed within a cabinet and that some of the Roman monuments were placed in the form of an antique alcove, covered with 'an Arch of Marble, of very curious Workmanship, which once belonged to a Shrine in the Lady's Chapel

at York Minster… The fore part of the Alcove is adorned with antique Woodwork, Coat of Arms etc… from Glastonbury Abbey: And above them all IHS (Greek for Jesus) crowned in raised work'.[89]

Ralph's skill, particularly as a numismatist, brought him to the attention of some of the most notable antiquaries and dilettanti of the age, including Sir John Evelyn, Sir Christopher Wren, Sir Hans Sloane, Rev. William Nicholson, Thomas Hearne and Dr Edmund Gibson. Indeed many prestigious visitors came to Leeds to view his collections, including Lord Fairfax, Lord Irwin, Dr John Sharp, the Archbishop of York, members of the local gentry and foreign dignitaries. This enhanced not only his own reputation but also that of the town. Indeed, in 1697 in recognition of his work he had been elected a Fellow of the Royal Society — a huge achievement for a provincial merchant's son whose formal education had gone no further than a few years at a tiny local grammar school.

Thoresby was 67 when he died on 16 October 1725. Sadly his family showed no interest in his life's work. While his eldest son Ralph, soon to be Rector of Stoke Newington near London, took the valuable items, including his coin collection, medals, manuscripts, books and autographs to his home, the bulk of the collection was left to rot until 1743 'so they became like a Dunghill'.

Ralph Thoresby's House

Thoresby's house, (PB) key opposite.

There was already a timber-framed house dated 1508 on the plot (**A**) when John the elder purchased the property. This was too small and unimposing for a wealthy cloth merchant and so John built a sizable extension to the building (**B**). This was further enlarged in 1653 when a gabled extension was built to the rear (**C**). The house now consisted of an elegant drawing room, breakfast room, library, study and various bedrooms. Fresh, pure water came from the draw well (**D**) in the yard at the back.

John died on 20 September 1661 and his son, John the younger (1625-1679), Ralph's father, inherited the property, including a large stable block and kitchen (**E**), above which he kept his embryonic museum. Ralph inherited the property in 1679 and at some point an observatory (**F**) was added to the roof of the main house, where he could pursue his interest in astronomy and enjoy the magnificent views across the town to Kirkstall Abbey to the west and the moors of Chapel Allerton and Potternewton to the north. Fire was a constant hazard in timber-framed buildings and Ralph had several narrow escapes from disaster, so in 1678 he paid workmen to build a new fireplace with a huge brick chimney stack (**G**).[90]

More space was required to accommodate his growing collection and in 1692 Ralph was fortunate enough to purchase a long tongue of land that abutted his stables, and had easy access to Vicar Lane, from Nicholas Bickerdyke (1637-1701), a wealthy haberdasher of Norwich.[91] This land parcel had originally been part of Ralph's grandfather's estate but had been sold by his Uncle Timothy (d.1670) to raise money to help ease his financial difficulties. Bickerdyke had built a stylish tall tower (**H**) on the eastern edge of his property, where he took clients to discuss business. Once Ralph had acquired the plot he erected a brick building to house part of his museum (**I**). The gabled structure was supported on an arched colonnade (**J**). Above the door to his library he incorporated one of the magnificent gothic niches from the shrine of St William at York Minster (**K**). This development also included a number of dwellings to rent (**L**), thereby bringing him a regular income to supplement the diminishing returns from his ailing cloth business. Arguably the most important room of all was Ralph's study (**M**) where he wrote his diaries, the Review of his life 1658-1714, the *Ducatus Leodiensis* (1715) and the *Vicaria Leodiensis*, the history of Leeds Parish Church which he published in 1724.

On 10 October 1724, when he was in poor health, Ralph made another version of his will.[92] That month he was 'struck with a violent palsy' but recovered enough to speak and walk unaided. Nevertheless when Edward Haley (1689-1741) 2nd Earl of Oxford, the well-known politician, bibliophile, collector and patron of the arts visited the museum he noted that Ralph was 'so old, so decayed, infirm and decrepit that one could have been content not to have seen [him]'.[93]

Thoresby's home in Kirkgate, his fine library, manuscript collection and vast museum with its valuable coins and medals, were to be given to his eldest son, Ralph junior, then Vicar of Rickmansworth. That same month Ralph's finances were becoming desperate and eleven months later the following advert appeared in the *Leeds Mercury*:

> To be Sold. Two good Houses in Kirkgate, Leeds, one in the occupation of Mr. John Wood, the other adjoining thereto on the West side, late of the occupation of John Dickinson; another House on the Backside thereof, with a large Yard, a convenient Stable, Outhouses and Garden and also another House now in two dwellings with a Stable in Vicar Lane, and adjoining to the said Houses and Tenements in Kirkgate. Enquire of Mr Ralph Thoresby aforesaid.[94]

Despite repeated adverts there were no takers and on 16 October 1725 he died aged 68. He was buried three days later at his beloved parish church, St Peter's.[95]

Thoresby's house was located in one of the most desirable parts of town but by this date it was old-fashioned and not in the Palladian style that had become so popular.[96] Its sale was further complicated by Ralph's apparent desire to let his wife, Anna, remain living there until her death. She was to outlive him by sixteen years. It is clear that she had no real interest in the museum or the library which fell rapidly into disrepair. Ralph junior transported the most valuable items, including the coins, medals and manuscripts, to his home in Rickmansworth almost immediately but in April 1728 he was appointed Rector of Stoke Newington, near London, and with a fine rectory felt able to take delivery of more material. Anna left the rest of the collection to rot, while Ralph's protégé, James Lucas, the local schoolmaster, desperately tried to find potential buyers; some unscrupulous people like Dr Burton stole as much as they purchased! They rifled the collection, some of which, like the stones, minerals and salts had 'lain in a Garret like a Heap of Rubbish from 1726 to 1743, the rain, snow etc... beating in on all sides'.[97]

Leaving Thoresby's property, just below, on the opposite side of the street, we would have reached the grand house of James Ibbetson, whose family was obsessed with money and trade. On Cossins' Plan it was James Ibbetson's coat of arms that was emblazoned next to that of Lord Irwin and the Borough of Leeds. Ibbetson's house, illustrated in the margin of the plan, was five bays wide and three storeys high with a basement lit by semi-circular windows. The impressive entrance immediately showed visitors that they were entering the home of a man of wealth. The wide double doors with a fanlight above were sheltered by a portico with classical urns above the entablature and below the roof was a deep mullioned cornice.

Ibbetson's House on Cossins' Plan.

Their house abutted the street and was ideally located between the traditional cloth market held on Briggate, and the new White Cloth Hall. The Ibbetsons had been relatively humble clothiers and clothworkers in the town since the sixteenth century but through hard work and guile had prospered. James, who died in 1673, was the first to be classed as a merchant. His status in the local community was reflected in his impressive newly-built house on this site. His second son, Samuel, inherited the house along with a further £150 to enable additional enhancement work to be undertaken. Thoresby had joined Samuel in a business enterprise, crushing rape-seed in a mill at Sheepscar to produce oil that was used by dry-

salters and clothiers in the preparatory processes of wool yarn manufacture. The venture was a spectacular failure and, before his early death in 1697, Samuel cunningly offloaded the very large debts incurred on to the naïve Thoresby.

Ralph's hatred of Samuel's son and heir, James (1674-1739), stemmed from his steadfast refusal to repay to him his father's share of the debts despite the fact that by the 1720s he had become a spectacularly successful merchant making the family one of the very wealthiest in the town. When he had inherited his father's estate in 1697 it would appear that the house was being remodelled but, ever conscious of demonstrating the family's improved status, he had completely rebuilt it again in 1715.[98]

Kirkgate was an extremely pleasant place to live and its ambience was improving year by year in the second decade of the eighteenth century. Diagonally opposite to the Ibbetson house, at the junction of Vicar Lane and Kirkgate, was Vicar's Croft and the vicarage (today the site of Kirkgate Market). In this large field, given to the parish church in 1453 by William Scot de Newton, had stood the late medieval vicarage. The Reverend Joseph Cookson (1678-1745), the new vicar and the younger brother of the merchant William Cookson, had decided that the old vicarage was outdated and no longer reflected his social standing in an increasingly prosperous town of around 6000 people. After less than a year as the new vicar of Leeds, he had rebuilt it as a five bay, three-storey brick mansion in the latest fashionable style.

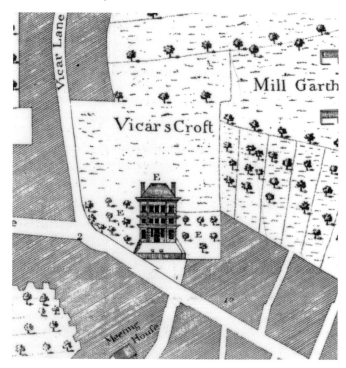

The Vicar's Croft on Cossins' Plan.

Rev. Joseph Cookson (1678-1725). (Private Collection Photo © Christie's Images/Bridgeman Images)

Indeed this was the era in which the wealthy merchant residents of Kirkgate were replacing what they now regarded as 'old-fashioned' timber-framed houses with modern Palladian-style town houses with which contemporary visitors to London, York or Bath would have been familiar. Below the vicarage, John Berkenhold of Hamburg and Bernard Bischoff, an immigrant from Basle, both successful merchants, had erected the fine new brick houses shown in the margins of Cossins' plan. We cannot be sure of the precise position of Berkenhold's almost palatial eleven-bayed, three storey house but the watercolour of Kirkgate in 1803 on page 63 suggest the large houses just below Vicar's Croft on the left.

Berkenhold's House on Cossins' Plan.

Progressing down the southern side of Kirkgate, we would have come to the First White Cloth Hall. In 1710, as we have seen, this site had been occupied by the ancient fabric of the chantry priest's house and a row of ruinous old almshouses. Cossins' plan shows us that Mr Bischoff's grand new house stood directly opposite.

Bischoff's House on Cossins' Plan.

As we shall see later, it was one of the best appointed merchant houses in Leeds being ideally situated for the Cloth Hall and it had the advantage of a long yard and croft extending behind to a depth of 390 feet.

After pointing out the decaying almshouses, Thoresby somewhat regretfully observed that 'Abutting hereupon is the cippus [that is the leg stocks] of the Lord Irwin's Manor of Kirkgate'; notwithstanding the growing elegance of the Kirkgate merchants' homes and lifestyle, the eighteenth century was still a brutal era: the magistrates of Leeds not infrequently sentenced male and female malefactors to be whipped up and down Briggate 'till their backs be bloody'.

Going further down Kirkgate, just beyond the corner of what is today Wharf Street (then a cart track), we would have come to the 'good old-fashioned' timber-framed houses of the Cooksons and the Pawsons, and finally the Kirkgate manor house, behind which still stands the medieval tithe barn — a massive wooden structure where the courts of the manor of Kirkgate were still held.[99]

Pawson's and Cookson's timber-framed houses on Kirkgate. (Leeds Library and Information Services)

At the bottom end of Kirkgate we would have arrived at the parish church, for Thoresby the greatest public building in the town. 'The Parish-Church', he wrote in *Ducatus,* 'is a very spacious and strong Fabrick, and Emblem of the Church Militant, black but comely, being of great Antiquity; it doth not pretend to the Mode of Reformed Architecture, but is strong and useful ... plain but

venerable... [and] built after the manner of a cathedral.' He noted that it was filled with 'monuments and banners and escutcheons' and then devoted many pages to describing them, their inscriptions and the families associated with them.

Again the vitality of Leeds in 1710-25 is very striking, with the improvement of the town a recurrent theme. In the addenda to the *Ducatus* Thoresby excitedly reports the great news that about 1710, the church had undergone a tremendous renovation and beautification. No longer does he regard it as merely 'black but comely'. 'The Parish Church', he says, 'does now flourish as a bride adorned with her jewels; and although the altars might be more pompous in the times of Popery, we may safely conclude that the entire church was never more beautiful since its foundation.' Alderman Cookson had become church warden and a dramatic change had resulted: the windows had been re-glazed, the choir of the church had a new ceiling, a fine

Parish Church chancel looking west from the altar, by John N. Rhodes. (Leeds Library and Information Services)

organ had been installed and there had been a complete redecoration. The celebrated French artist Monsieur James Parmentier had painted a vast work to adorn the high altar. Thoresby recorded that he had 'bestowed upon the Church a most noble Specimen of his Art, viz. the Giving of the Law, the Thunder and Lightning at the rending of the thick Clouds are expressed (in a fresco upon the Roof) in suitable Terror, but qualified by the lovely aspects of a Choir of Angels and Cherubs with Moses and Aaron in the Clouds etc...'[100]

Parmentier's (1658-1730) talent was such that he had been invited by William III to decorate his palace at Het Loo near the Hague, undertook work for Thomas Howard, 8th Duke of Norfolk, at Worksop Manor in Nottinghamshire, and for Charles Howard, 3rd Earl of Carlisle at Castle Howard. He gained many commissions from the merchants of Leeds including producing a series of historic paintings for Richard Wilson, the Recorder of Leeds, in a room in his house at Mill Hill.

Not all merchants chose to live on a bustling thoroughfare. The end of our tour takes us into The Calls, at this time a relatively peaceful and beautiful backwater. Thoresby noted that 'From the Church to the Bridge is the Foot Pathway thro' the Fields by certain Gardens (particularly, Alderman Cookson's who has lately erected here a very pleasant seat [i.e. a house] with Terras Walks etc) which is yet named the Calls or Cawls.' This wonderful new Cookson mansion, carefully depicted on the face of Cossins' plan, had been erected around 1710 by William Cookson the elder (1639-1716), while he lived in the old timber-framed house on Kirkgate. He had built it for his son Alderman William Cookson (1669-1743), who was thrice mayor of Leeds in 1712, 1725 and 1738.

Cookson Mansion on Cossins' Plan.

William Cookson (1669-1743). He married well, securing as a bride Susannah, the daughter of another incomer, Michael Idle (1630-97), a fellow merchant of Meadow Lane, who had been mayor in 1690. Unfortunately their first three children died in infancy and it was their fourth child, John, born in 1706, who eventually survived to adulthood. (Private Collection Photo © Christie's Images/Bridgeman Images)

It was testimony to the success of the Cookson dynasty. Five bays in width and three storeys high, it was one of the finest houses in Leeds, it even had a viewing platform on the roof where family and visitors could admire the garden and the stunning views across the river and the Aire valley. As Cossins shows its beautiful formal terraced gardens were adorned with gazebos and bordered with delicate fencing. The garden straddled The Calls footpath and the southern portion extending to the riverbank featured another delicate fence with a third gazebo, there was even a small pleasure boat for use on the river.

The gardens were filled with a wide variety of trees, shrubs and plants.[101] Much to the anger of the Cooksons, sometimes the fruit proved too tempting to light fingered passers-by, as the local newspaper, the Leeds Mercury, revealed:

> Whereas Ald. Cookson's garden, joining upon the River, was robb'd on Sunday Night the 20th Instant… and a great Numbers of Peaches, Nectarines, and Pears, taken away, supposed to be done by Persons coming from Halton Feast. If anyone will give Information thereof that one or more Persons may be convicted he shall receive a Guinea Reward.[102]

Here Monsieur James Parmentier had also worked his art, painting portraits of the family, both past and present, including 'Grandfather, Grandmother, Father, Mother and Uncle' for display in the dining room.[103] The house had a fine library, another mark of the family's rising status.

There can be little doubt that though William Cookson the elder, the patriarch who was 71 by the time of the building of the new house, formally paid for it out of the profits of the family merchant business, it was his dynamic son William Cookson the younger (1669-1743), aged 51 by then, who was the driving force behind its design and erection. In the year the first copies of *Ducatus* were arriving in Leeds, William the younger had had a torrid time, for he had for a short time been imprisoned for suspected Jacobite sympathies. In August that year he had been unwell and travelled to Bath to take and bathe in the waters there. The following month he returned but as the English Jacobites had planned a rebellion in the West Country, his behaviour was viewed as suspicious. He was also accused of colluding with Sir William Wyndham, a Tory MP and suspected Jacobite. His Leeds mansion was searched and on 30 September he was arrested and sent to Newgate. He languished in gaol for six

months and was eventually bailed in April 1716.[104] He arrived back in Leeds the following month 'to the great joy of the generality of the Town'.[105]

William the elder, in his seventies and in failing health, was extremely worried; his son's dangerous political views posed a real threat to the family's future prosperity. He took the radical step of leaving half his estate, including the old house on Kirkgate where he was living, the new warehouse and property to the left of the main footpath to the riverside, to Joseph (1678-1746) his second son who had become vicar of Leeds in 1715. The other half, including the fine new mansion, he left to his nine year old grandson, John Cookson (b.1706), thus safeguarding his property from potential confiscation by the government.

John Cookson (1706-1783) shunned the life of a cloth merchant, became a barrister and moved away to Middlesex. He left his younger brother, Thomas, living in the mansion, administering the estate and carrying on the family cloth business. John never married and on his death in 1783 left most of his property to Thomas' eldest son, another William (1749-1811). (Private Collection Photo © Christie's Images/Bridgeman Images)

Thomas Cookson (1707-1773) became a member of the corporation in 1742 but resigned two years later. Around this time he employed Jonathan Richardson (c.1665-1745), one of the leading portrait painters of the age, to paint his portrait. (Roy Precious)

His father's subtle manoeuvres ring fenced the property but allowed William the younger to inherit his share of the business. He became even more successful than his father; having already been mayor of Leeds in 1712 he became so again in 1725 and 1738.

Ralph Thoresby loved The Calls and going along the footpath in the direction of the bridge, three fields beyond Cookson's garden, Cossins' plan shows a summerhouse named 'Thoresby's Folly'

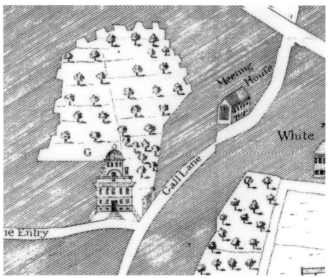

Call Lane Meeting House and Mr Atkinson's house and garden on Cossins' Plan.

at the foot of the tenter fields. This must surely have been the location of Thoresby's riverside garden that he created for himself in The Calls close to the river.

On 14 Feb 1681 he noted that there was a flood 'of prodigious greatness' in Leeds, the river water being so high that it brought large pieces of timber over his garden wall.[106] On 6 April 1682 he records: 'Was the whole day entirely at the new garden, by the water, overseeing workfolk, and reading Sir William Waller's Divine Meditations.......' On 17 April he noted: 'Rode with aunt Idle to Tong, to procure flowers for the new garden, of the noted florist there; but was severely wet, and not without danger in passing a small rivulet prodigiously risen with thundershowers, but got well home.'

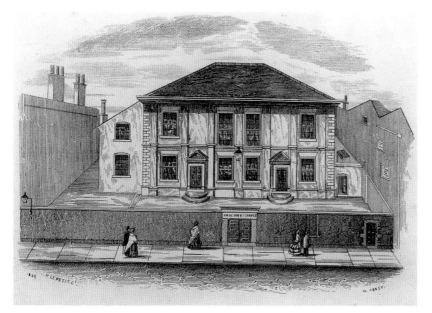

◄ *Call Lane Meeting House. This meeting house was built for the Independent Dissenters (or Arians) in 1691. It was built in brick and could seat a congregation of 530. It stood on the west side of Call Lane a few yards down from the junction with Kirkgate. (Engraver W. Askey)*

Mr Atkinson's House, John Russell watercolour 1803. (Photo © Birmingham Museums Trust)

Without doubt the grandest feature in the vicinity of The Calls and Call Lane in the early 1720s was the home of Mr Atkinson. Looking like a scaled-down Castle Howard, Cossins shows it with a large meadow behind as orchards or pleasure grounds. Thoresby in *Ducatus* tells us:

> In an orchard adjoining [Call Lane], where was lately the Grove and Summer-House of the noble benefactor Mr Harrison, the present proprietor John Atkinson Esq., Justice of the Peace for the West-Riding and Mayor of Leedes in 1711, is now building a delicate House, that for the exquisite Workmanship of the Stone-work, especially the Dome, and for a painted Stair-Case, excellently performed by Mons. Permentier, &c, exceeds all in Town.

Regrettably Mr Atkinson died in 1717 having had little time to enjoy his magnificent new house and its extensive grounds. At the time Cossins was preparing his town plan the house was being offered for sale, it being noted that its coach house would be suitable for a gentleman or as a packing shop for a merchant.[107] The small elevation on the plan shows the two storeys and basement, five bays wide with the dome above, but more detail can be seen in John Russell's wonderful watercolour painting of 1803. It had rusticated quoins at each end. The windows, with keystones in their arches, do not appear to be sashed, suggesting their considerable scale. The central window on the second floor had a semi-circular arch. Above the cornice the parapet hiding the roof was decorated with a central panel, topped by a segmental pediment between two square ornamental chimneys which framed the glorious colonnaded dome — a smaller Castle Howard indeed, and one can only imagine the splendour of Monsieur Parmentier's painted staircase.

Our walk comes to an end at the ancient bridge at the bottom of Briggate, just beyond the fording point where, in a sense, the story of Leeds and Kirkgate had begun.

Wealth beyond Measure: The 1770s

By the 1770s Leeds merchants handled a remarkable one-third of the vastly enlarged exports of woollen cloth from England to ports across Europe and, in particular, America. This was a vital service to the nation since this woollen cloth accounted for over half England's home-produced exports. In a good year in the 1770s exports of cloth from Leeds amounted to £1,500,000! The evidence of this huge growth in trade was writ large in Kirkgate with the First White Cloth Hall having been superseded in 1756 by the Second White Cloth Hall in Meadow Lane, and it in turn being replaced just over twenty years later by the much larger Third White Cloth Hall opened in 1777 on the tenter ground in The Calls.

Vast fortunes were generated in Leeds and its merchants became hugely influential, investing their new wealth in landed estates, transport improvements, government stock and the beautification of their homes with paintings by some of Europe's greatest artists including Rubens, Gainsborough, Reynolds and Stubbs. By far and away the most successful merchant was William Denison (1714-82) who had successfully exploited the Italian market. Despite the family's humble origins as clothiers at Great Woodhouse, a hamlet to the north of Leeds, his father that had made a fortune purchasing cloth in the halls of Leeds, Wakefield and Halifax. William built spectacularly on these firm foundations and from 1740 until 1782 he was the leading partner in the largest export house in Leeds. In 1781 alone, at a time when a worker's cottage might cost about £50, he had surplus funds of £20,000 to invest![108]

His Leeds home and business premises were conveniently located opposite the Assembly Rooms (the former First White Cloth Hall) and in 1777 the plot contained a house, counting house, packing shops, stable and coach-house, a garden, a close and a dung hill.[109] Unlike many of his contemporaries Denison shunned public office, refusing on four occasions to serve as mayor. He concentrated on his business and the accumulation of wealth, including annuities and government stock. He invested much of the profits from the business in buying estates in Nottinghamshire and North Yorkshire and took a keen interest in agricultural improvements. He was a focused and driven man and, as a result, could afford an aristocratic lifestyle.

William Denison's house in Kirkgate (formerly owned by Mr. Bischoff). (PB) A ground floor plan of his house and croft is below.

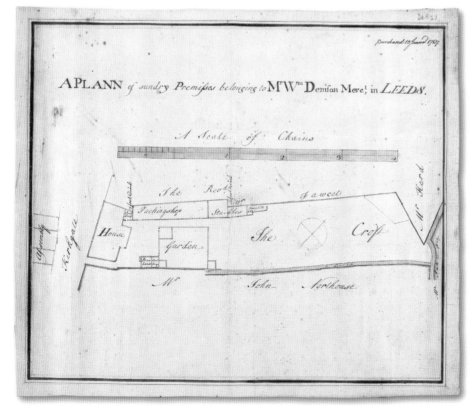

◄ *'A Plann of Sundry Premises belonging to Mr Wm Denison Merct. in Leeds, 13 January 1767'. (Manuscripts and Special Collections, University of Nottingham)*

When he felt dissatisfied with his portrait by Francis Cotes he could afford to secure the services of George Romney, one of the leading portrait painters of Georgian England, to improve upon it.[110]

In 1773 he became a partner in the London merchant house of Denison, Smith and Colebroke. His views were courted by everyone from aristocrats to politicians and his wealth ensured that he could holiday in style at Bath, the social centre of the national summer season. When he died in 1782 he is purported to have left his brother, Robert (1720-85), a fortune of £700,000, an amount worth well over £100 million today.[111]

Being the place of residence of such wealthy people, Kirkgate in the 1760s and 70s was now home to the makers of excellent wigs, marble fireplace manufacturers and suppliers of fine furniture. For those not as wealthy as William Denison, there were very pleasant but less grand houses to rent in Kirkgate. An advert in the Leeds Intelligencer on 15 June 1762 gives details of one of them:

> To be Lett to enter to at Pleasure, in Kirkgate, in Leedes. A large and convenient Dwellinghouse, wherein Mrs Ruth Dover lately dwelt, neatly fitted up with Paper-hanging, and Brass Locks to most of the Doors; with a Stable for two Horses and a Garden thereto belonging. For particulars enquire of Mr George Lumley, in Leedes, the Owner.[112]

There were good amenities too close at hand. On 1 November 1768 The Leeds Library opened in the back room of Joseph Ogle's bookshop at the sign of 'The Dial' at Kirkgate End. The eminent scientist Dr Joseph Priestley (1733-1804), who discovered oxygen and invented carbonated water, was its Secretary from 1768 to 1769 and President from 1769 to 1772. The library received enthusiastic support from the Leeds elite and in 1781 moved to rented accommodation in Sir James Ibbetson's former house.[113]

The glory of The Calls was the new Assembly Rooms above the Third White Cloth Hall. When Sir George Saville and Lady Effingham opened them on 9 June 1777 over two hundred gentlemen and ladies were 'very agreeably surprised at the neatness and elegance of the different apartments'. Admission for one gentleman and two ladies was half a guinea (far more than the ordinary worker could afford). Regular card and dancing assemblies were organised and the rooms were used for special events as well.

▲ Richard Mountain operated a fashionable shop with a 40 foot workshop, wood yard and saw pits in Kirkgate c. 1790-1800. (Redrawn by PB)

◄ The Assembly Rooms over the Third White Cloth Hall. (PB)

◄ William Denison (1714-82) by Francis Cotes (1726-1770) and George Romney (1734-1802). (The Museum of Fine Arts, Houston, The Renzi Collection, gift of Mr and Mrs Harris Masterson III)

The Fashionable Days of Kirkgate Come to an End

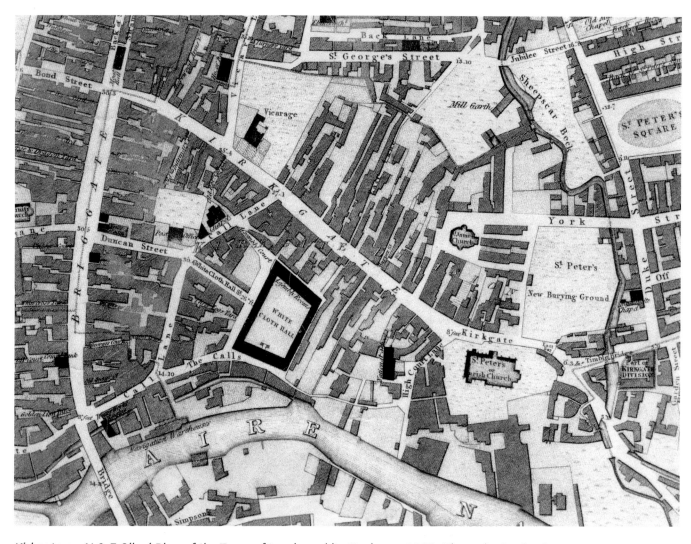

Kirkgate on N & F Giles' Plan of the Town of Leeds and its Environs, 1815. (Thoresby Society)

The plan of William Denison's Kirkgate property in 1777 shows us the contradiction which had arisen between the gentlemen merchants' aspirations for a genteel lifestyle and the pursuit of their rapidly expanding business activities. Merchants' finishing shops, warehouses and packing shops had traditionally been built in the yards behind their elegant homes. This permitted them close supervision of the finishing processes which added so much value of the cloth they sold and ensured that that quality was maintained. As business grew they needed to build more finishing and packing shops into their yards.

William Denison's quality of life would have suffered increasingly from not only the smell from his enormous dunghill but also the smoke from the chimneys of his and neighbouring houses and their finishing shops. Kirkgate became an increasingly busy thoroughfare with noise from people, carts, carriages and horses destroying the relative tranquillity that his predecessors had enjoyed.

Merchants who had previously relaxed in their gardens and used the fields behind their homes for leisure, the stretching of cloth on tenter frames and paddocks for their horses, began to use this space to generate additional income. Between 1700 and 1770 the population of Leeds rose by 10,000 to around 17,000. Since no new streets were built, the burgeoning ranks of the lower orders were accommodated by building cottages in the yards, gardens and orchards behind the main street frontages, with owners benefiting from the lucrative rents.[114] In 1740 there were 305 properties listed on Kirkgate with 194 rated at under £2. This was to rise to around 800 houses by 1775.[115] Thus Kirkgate witnessed the construction of many 'blind-back' working class cottages and lodging houses which landlords squeezed into the narrow plots extending from the street.

Typical of this change was the development of the croft behind the Boot and Shoe Inn, located on the north side of Kirkgate close to the vicarage. In

1767 the croft contained only a single warehouse but only three years later twelve newly-built one-room cottages in it were advertised for sale, and by 1795 a further ten had been added.[116] Lacking decent sanitary arrangements and plagued by negligible access to clean water, overcrowded 'backsides' such as these were to become the fever dens of the town. Public houses were erected along with shops, workshops, cottages and lodging houses to cater for the needs of the growing population. In 1774 the Kirkgate Ward of the town contained one-fifth of the town's cheapest houses and these constituted two-fifths of the property of the district.[117]

Old Infirmary Yard.
(Leeds Library and Information Services)

For the moment at least, the wealthy still lived cheek by jowl with the working classes – there was no segregation – and they were acutely aware of the plight of the poor. In 1767 the first Leeds Infirmary for the sick poor opened in Andrew Wilson's house in a yard off Kirkgate,[118] and in the severe winter of 1780-1 William Denison distributed flour and coals to every poor inhabitant of the street.[119] However, as its

environment deteriorated and it became more crowded, the area became much less desirable as a place to live for the very wealthy and they moved out.

An excellent example of this process of change is provided by the Cookson family. As we have seen, when John Cookson (1706-1783) inherited the estate of his father William Cookson junior in 1743, he was already a successful London barrister and had no interest in returning to Leeds. Instead he allowed his brother, Thomas (1707-1773), to live in the fine mansion house off Kirkgate and run their business affairs from there. Thomas died in 1773 but his son, William (1749-1811), continued living in the house for another five years and there enjoyed the lifestyle of a successful cloth merchant. When he married Mary Scott in 1778 they moved to a stylish new eleven-bedroomed house of their own on South Parade, part of the fashionable new Park Estate developing on the west side of the town. In 1783 John Cookson (the barrister) died and William inherited his uncle's estate including the mansion house which was by now old-fashioned and redundant. It had been leased out to Lady Milner but he continued to use its outbuildings for his cloth business.

Now that William was living in style elsewhere, he cared little for the fate of the beautiful old garden in The Calls and set about developing its commercial potential. Since the opening of the Aire and Calder Navigation in 1699, river traffic had increased seven-fold and the demand for new wharves and warehouses ensured that owners of such facilities were guaranteed a good return on their investment. William paid for the piling of the river bank in the lower section of the garden. This became a coal staithe which he immediately leased to Thomas Fenton, the 'Coal King', for landing coal from his new mines at Rothwell Haigh. He then converted part of the upper garden into a timber yard.[120]

Despite the deterioration of the environment around her, Lady Milner lived in the mansion until her death in 1788, aged 86. The contents of the house, including three sets of hangings which she had for the furniture of each bed, were sold by Thomas Stooks the auctioneer.[121] In 1791 the house ceased to be occupied as a home and was then subdivided and used for industrial purposes. This change of use both reflected and contributed to the decline of Kirkgate.

Barstow's Mansion opposite the parish church. (Leeds Library and Information Services)

By the late 1770s lavish residences in the latest style were no longer built in Kirkgate, giving way to the construction of modest and functional buildings. The large site next to the First White Cloth Hall, once an ideal position for a merchant's residence was subdivided by Richard Lawson and developed as 'Four New-built Dwelling Houses, fronting the Street'. Unfortunately he had overstretched himself and in 1777 was declared bankrupt.[122]

Many of the wealthiest residents leaving the area leased out their mansions or sub-divided them to maximize profit, before moving to the fashionable Park Estate or to the smoke-free villages of Potternewton, Chapel Allerton and Headingley on the northern plateau. It is significant that the substantial house advertised for renting in the *Leeds Intelligencer* in the mid-1770s by then had part of its frontage converted to a shop:

To be Lett, a very good and Convenient Sashed Dwelling-House, situate in Kirkgate, Leeds, which Mr Benjamin Dawson, Surgeon, lately inhabited. The House consists of a Shop and a large Dining Room in the Front, a Kitchen, and a large Room Backwards, two good Cellars, four Chambers, three large Closets, and three Garrets: Five Rooms and the Stair-Case are hung with Paper and the whole is in very good condition; there are Grates fixed in all the Rooms, and a good Smoke-Jack in the Kitchen. For Particulars inquire of Mr Benjamin Dawson at Mr Kenion's Shop in Boar-Lane.[123]

In March 1773 the following advert appeared:

To be Lett, a Genteel sash'd Messuage, having three large Bow windows facing towards Chappel-Town and Gledhow, with a commodious Court before and pleasant Garden behind the same, situate in Kirkgate, Leeds, adjoining to where Doctor Hird now dwells, and lately occupied by Mr. Thomas Barstow; consisting of nine neat Rooms from the Ground Floor; a good low Kitchen, Pantry, Scullery, two arch'd Cellars, with Privilege to wash and brew in the Common Brewhouse in the Yard; Also a Hay Chamber and a three Stall Stable in the Yard. Apply to Mr. John Moxon, Attorney at Law at his office in Briggate.[124]

Kirkgate in 1803. This watercolour was painted by John Russell on a visit to Leeds. The centre of the view is dominated by the medieval Leeds parish church but is framed on the left by the stone wall of Vicar's Croft and on the right by the impressive Ibbetson mansion. The Ibbetsons had rebuilt or substantially altered the house several times. On the last occasion in 1752, with John Carr as the architect, they extended its front into the street, 5 feet 5 inches beyond the normal building line, much to the anger of their neighbours! Just below, partly concealed by the projecting front of the Ibbetson house, we can see eight-bays of another three-storey merchant house; perhaps this had been Mr Berkenhold's 11-bayed house shown on Cossins' Plan? Further down on the right a low, possibly single-storey building stands at the junction with Call Lane. Opposite Call Lane is another fine merchant house with at least seven bays. (Photo © Birmingham Museums Trust)

As the advert notes the wealthy lawyer Thomas Barstow, who was later town clerk in 1781 and 1792, had occupied this fine house opposite the parish church but had eventually succumbed to the charms of a residence in Park Row away from the constant cacophony of sound from the congested, noisy street and the increasing number of people from the lower orders who frequented its alleys and yards. Even the close proximity to St Peter's could no longer make this a highly desirable street for the most wealthy. Conditions deteriorated still further by the end of the century creating a situation ably summarised by the writer of *The Leeds Guide* in 1806:

'If we were to estimate the importance of streets by the number of inhabitants they contain, Kirkgate would certainly claim distinguished notice, as it is extremely populace. But as fashionable people, and with them fashionable tradesmen, have deserted it, this street is fallen into some kind of disrepute, and if it did not happen to be the road to the Church, it would be a place, to adopt a fashionable phrase, which nobody knew; but as it is a wide, and upon the whole a well-built street, it may probably at some future period recover its former consequence'.[125]

Development of the Manor House Site

Kirkgate showing the Manor House, the Pawson property and the Cookson residence. (Leeds Library and Information Services)

This historically valuable photograph taken in in 1909 is one image that encapsulates the development of Kirkgate from its Anglo-Saxon origins to the end of the eighteenth century. It shows the edge of the parish churchyard and the frontage of the Viking thegns' hall enclosure (A to B). This lay between the present-day High Court Lane (the minor road beyond the railings) and Wharf Street (just before the railway viaduct). In the Anglo-Saxon period the Christian missionary centre was established within a ditched enclosure (1). After the Norman Conquest when the manor was given to the Alien Benedictine monks of Holy Trinity, York, they built a manor house as an administrative centre (2). In Tudor times the majority of Kirkgate's residents were clothiers and clothworkers. One of the most successful was John Pawson who lived in a timber-framed house near the church (3).

During the seventeenth century the cloth-making industry prospered and ambitious immigrants arrived in the town seeking their fortune, these included William Cookson who lived in a much larger five-bay timber-framed house (4) which he extended to accommodate his growing family and successful business as a cloth merchant. The riches generated by the cloth trade allowed the growing merchant community to build elegant Palladian town houses in Kirkgate, filled with all the trappings of wealth, from oil paintings to fine silver. The Pawsons, for example, rose from clothier to merchant class, purchased the plot next to their old house and built a fine four-

bay, three-storey brick house (5) in the latest fashionable style.

Yet by the early nineteenth century this elegant age had passed. The former manor house (2) was subdivided, creating four shop units with living accommodation above.

When Anne Norcliffe Dalton (nee Pawson) died in 1801 the last link between this ancient family and Kirkgate was severed. The original Tudor house (3) had for years been the Old Crown Inn but now the Georgian family house (5) was sub-divided into shops with accommodation above and became nothing other than a source of income for her heirs, who had no sentimental attachment to the property. The Cooksons had been extremely successful in securing a succession of wealthy tenants for their old timber-framed house (4) but when the widow of John Sturgess, former Excise Officer and one of the founders of the Bowling Iron Works, died in 1796, no such tenant could be found. By this date the social elite of Leeds had migrated to the Park Estate or to the villages of Headingley, Potternewton and Chapel Allerton abandoning what had once been one of the most prestigious locations in the town. Their old family house was also sub-divided and converted into commercial premises with shop fronts erected at ground level. Moreover the 'backsides' of so many of these Kirkgate properties had become crowded with cottages for the working classes and lodging houses for the ever increasing number of migrant workers seeking employment in the rapidly expanding town.

The range of buildings shown in the photograph was demolished in 1933-1934 as part of a major road improvement scheme. Unfortunately no recording of these important buildings or archaeological excavation took place and a unique opportunity to reveal the origin of Leeds and chart its evolution was lost.

Kirkgate Today

Kirkgate from the air. Aerial view © Bluesky Ltd. <2009> © Crown copyright and database rights 2016 Ordnance Survey 100019567

Since the late 1980s much of the core of Leeds city centre's retail district has undergone a remarkable regeneration and transformation acquiring the title of 'The Knightsbridge of the North'. The break in this caused by the Credit Crunch of 2008 and the ensuing economic recession has now been overcome and renewal has gathered considerable pace again with the opening of the Trinity Centre in 2013 and the Victoria Gate shopping centre with the largest John Lewis store outside London set to open in the autumn of 2016. And yet Kirkgate has been untouched by this private sector investment.

While the Corn Exchange, part of the Third White Cloth Hall behind it and the Edwardian Kirkgate Market Hall were wonderfully renovated in the 1990s, in public perception the properties of Lower Kirkgate, above all on the south side, have seemingly been left untouched — a complete affront to the potential of the city's first street. The 1806 Leeds Guide's comment, that 'this street is fallen into some kind of disrepute' and that 'if it did not happen to be the road to the Church it would be a place which nobody [wished to know]', seems almost as apt today as it did just over two hundred years ago.

How pleasing it is then that the setting up of the Lower Kirkgate Townscape Heritage Initiative in

2012, with the support of the Heritage Lottery Fund, Leeds City Council, English Heritage, and Leeds Civic Trust, demonstrates that people again do want to know Kirkgate and secure its regeneration based on celebrating its heritage. Kirkgate can become one of the gems of Leeds and a significant visitor attraction. The proposed regeneration can restore, mend and polish the largely Georgian south side of the street and, through critically important archaeological investigation, tell us much that we cannot learn by any other means about the origins the city. The British people of the Kingdom of Elmet, the Anglo-Saxons, the Vikings and the Normans all lived in Leeds over the ages, and it was in Kirkgate and the vicinity of Leeds Minster that they lived. No opportunity for the archaeological investigation of Kirkgate must be lost.

In many ways it is remarkable that a substantial part of the First White Cloth Hall survives today. Deceived by John Cossins' Plan showing the cloth hall as being well set back from the Kirkgate frontage down a long alley, people assumed it had been demolished. Then in 1983 an English Heritage officer making a random inspection of some old buildings in Kirkgate noted when he got inside that behind the main frontage there was a courtyard, which though much altered, clearly had once had had a series of arches on its ground floor. The First White Cloth Hall had been rediscovered! Schemes to restore the building have come and gone over the last thirty years, and inaction and failure to repair its fabric led to the collapse of the west wing in 2010. The condition of the building is now so poor that a significant point has been reached. The opportunity through the Townscape Heritage Initiative may be the building's last chance to be saved.

There is significant potential for above and below ground archaeology in the Kirkgate area. New development goes hand in hand with archaeological investigation. This investigation of the below ground remains could give an important glimpse of medieval Leeds which in 2016 is still obscure.

The First White Cloth Hall as it appeared in the ▶ *Edwardian period. The hipped roofs of the wings of the Cloth Hall are clearly seen above the frontages of 98 and 100 Kirkgate. By this time the front of the central courtyard had been infilled.*

The First White Cloth Hall in 1984 just after it had been given listed building status.

The west wing of the First White Cloth Hall being demolished in 2010.

The First White Cloth Hall in 2015. This picture shows the east wing of the Cloth Hall with its infilled ground floor arcading visible with vegetation growing in the courtyard. By this time the east wing had been demolished. The adjacent Georgian Hill's Furnishings was still standing but was demolished shortly after as a result of the fire in December 2015.

The charred remains of the panelling of the late Tudor/early seventeenth century building behind Hill's Furnishings which was destroyed by fire in December 2015. See also the illustration on page 14.

The First White Cloth Hall is an opportunity for such investigation given its long occupation already mentioned earlier in this book. In November 2015 a fire at Hill's Furnishings shop on Kirkgate resulted in the demolition of both Hill's and the gutted and charred remains of the substantial building or buildings behind. The very sad loss of the Georgian merchant's house which Hill's occupied was compounded by the revelation that the buildings behind dated from the late Middle Ages and the late Tudor/early seventeenth century period. Very large ancient timber roof trusses and beams survived the fire and, before the demolition of the gutted charred structure, substantial sections of high quality wooden panelling could be seen. A small section of exquisitely decorated timber panel suggests that part of the structure may have belonged to the chantry priest's house (see page 14). These discoveries, in regrettable circumstances, demonstrate this historic street still has many surprises yet to be revealed.

A timber core sample being taken of a beam from the building behind Hill's Furnishings to establish its date by dendrochronology. Some of the timbers were found to be of the mid-15th century and could well be part of the chantry priest's house. These were incorporated into a fine early 17th century building which had elegant panelled rooms. ▼

View of Kirkgate in 2010 looking towards Leeds Parish Church.

The south side of Lower Kirkgate in March 2016. Despite the poor condition of the buildings, a revival has begun. The first building on the left has been renovated internally by East Street Arts for an 'Art Hostel'. Higher up, no. 92 has been fully renovated as the Wapentake bakery and café/bar. Artists have reclaimed part of the Kirkgate area with galleries in the nearby Wharf Chambers on Wharf Street and Fred Aldous (art and craft supplies) has occupied no. 34 Kirkgate.

Poundworld and SuperCards, with its purple sign, today occupy the site of Ralph Thoresby's house. SuperCards is the site of the bricked-fronted east end of his house (see the watercolour on page 45; the adjacent four-storey no. 19 still stands today).

Wapentake: a fine renovation for a bakery and bar.

The grey-fronted Creative Hair shop and the three shops to its right are the four 'New-built Dwelling Houses' erected by Richard Lawson in the 1770s. See page 62.

The work of the Townscape Heritage Initiative Team with the backing of a number of individuals and organisations has begun to bear fruit. In December 2015 the owners of no. 92 Kirkgate, the first to take advantage of the grant regime, opened the doors of their beautifully renovated Georgian premises as The Wapentake bakery and bar/restaurant. The transformation of the building has demonstrated powerfully how splendid these sad, rundown buildings of Kirkgate can look when renovated. Lower down the street next to Leeds Minster, encouraged by the new interest in Kirkgate, another Georgian building with an uncertain future has been splendidly renovated by the Leeds Brewery as The Lamb and Flag public house.

At present the future of the highly important First White Cloth Hall still hangs in the balance. The huge historic significance of the building has been clearly demonstrated in this book. The value of renovating its extant fabric and reconstructing those parts which have been demolished is clear. This building, which has played such an important role in promoting the economic success of the city, should once again become an emblem of Leeds and the flagship of a regenerated Kirkgate.

The Lamb and Flag pub — a regeneration success.

The Reconstruction Drawings: How were they done?

One of our great ambitions and challenges in writing this book has been to use our skills as researchers, historians and writers to bring both the people of Kirkgate's past back to life and, where possible, to recreate its buildings and streetscape. In over forty years of research we have amassed many small fragments of evidence about the physical character of Kirkgate over the centuries; it is thanks to the brilliance of Peter Brears in visually interpreting this evidence that this book contains several remarkable reconstruction images. So that these images will not be viewed as mere flights of fancy, below we provide details of some of the more important pieces of evidence used in their creation.

There are six key reconstruction pictures. The sources for creating two of them — John Pawson's house and the seventeenth century bakehouse found in the cellar of number 8 Kirkgate — have already been described in the main body of the book; the evidence for the other four — the picture of the manor of Kirkgate in 1089, the manor bakehouse and Hall of Pleas, and the two of Ralph Thoresby's house — is discussed below.

The Manor of Kirkgate in 1089

In the absence of any significant archaeological investigation of Kirkgate, it is map and documentary evidence which has provided the principal basis for the depiction of the manor of Kirkgate in 1089 — the year when it came into the possession of Holy Trinity Priory, York. Ancient field and property boundaries remain written in the landscape over many centuries and were shaped by natural features such as streams as is clearly the case with Kirkgate. The plan of Kirkgate underpinning this painting was based on Steven's careful tracing of the features hidden in the 6 inch to the mile Ordnance Survey map of 1847. These shapes in the landscape were deciphered through forensic comparison with other key maps, principally Cossins' Plan of 1726, the West Yorkshire Archive Service's map relating to Leeds (King's) Mills (WYL 160/234/4), Francis and Netlam Giles' Plan of Leeds in 1815, Fowler's Plan of the Kirkgate Ward in 1844 and the Goad Plans of 1886. The original alignment of Call Lane with the former fording point of the River Aire was clearly apparent on the Ordnance Survey map and was confirmed by aerial photographs. Leeds Bridge (later built higher up the river) aligns with Briggate and must have been built in association with the creation of the manorial borough in 1207; indeed the first reference to the bridge is in the 1322-1327 accounts of the Keeper of Rebels' Lands in Yorkshire for the Manor of Leeds (see J. le Patourel, Manor and Borough of Leeds, 1066-1400 [Leeds, 1957] pp. 12-27).

The curious present-day bend in Call Lane, which sharply changes direction at its lower end, must have been created to take traffic to and from the bridge. The fact that the track, later known as Call Lane, passes through a large enclosure suggests that originally this was not a busy routeway. The Calls, which led to the church, manor house, tithe barn and York, crossed no such enclosure, instead hugging the bank of the river before heading north beneath Quarry Hill.

The location, shape and size of the Kirkgate manor house was revealed by a contemporary marginal note in a draft of Ralph Thoresby's *Ducatus* held in the York Minster Archive, the Sale Particulars and Plan of Shops and Dwelling Houses on Kirkgate (WYAS: Leeds WYL 59/56) and Street Work Plan No 20 and two other estate plans contained in the deed parcels relating to Leeds Corporation Act, 1924 held by Leeds City Council's Legal Services. The scale of the original church site is clearly shown on the Cossins' Plan and the map associated with the proposed widening of Kirkgate in 1819 (WYAS: Leeds RDP68/38). The ditch surrounding the churchyard is mentioned in the medieval documents relating to 'The Leeds Fight', see E. K. Clark, 'A Brawl in Kirkgate', Thoresby Society, IV (1895), pp. 125-138.

Historians today are finding convincing physical evidence of the planning of medieval villages, as opposed to the former assumption that they developed randomly. Often, however, no documentary evidence survives to indicate when a regular grid pattern for villagers' holdings along streets were either agreed or imposed. Elements of a planned layout for part of the village of Leeds are evident on the southern side of Kirkgate just below the junction with Call Lane. Our attention was first drawn to this area by the curious 'back lane' that was visible on the Cossins' Plan and is still a feature of the townscape today as the road still abuts the northern wall of the Third White Cloth Hall. Careful measurement of this area has enabled us to identify four distinct plots based on a width of 29 feet for a single plot and 58 feet for a double-width plot. These plots have a depth of around 136 feet. One of the double plots is today occupied by the First White Cloth Hall.

The narrow thin plots to the north of Kirkgate were, quite clearly, former medieval farming strips fossilised in the plan of the settlement. The open field which contained the vicarage is readily apparent on Cossins' Plan and the detailed plans of the Kirkgate Market estate. To the west, from Vicar Lane to Briggate, there is evidence of the burgage plots that were created in 1207 along with Briggate; these matched the record of five burgage plots on Kirkgate which are referred to in surviving medieval documents (see J. Kirkby, The Manor and Borough of Leeds, 1425-1662, Thoresby Society, LV11 [Leeds, 1983], p. xxxiv). Four of these appear on the north side and include the site of the Golden Cock Inn and Ralph Thoresby's house and at least one, later known as Infirmary Yard, appears on the south side. The sale plan of The Golden Cock Hotel (WYAS: Leeds WYL 59/204) proved particularly useful in determining the northern and western bounds of the burgage plots.

The Manorial Bakehouse and Hall of Pleas
Peter's reconstruction picture of the medieval bakehouse and Hall of Pleas is based on the detailed account of the expenses incurred in the repair of this building which appear in the Manor of Leeds Reeve's Account for the period Michaelmas 1438 to Michaelmas 1439 (see J. Kirkby, The Manor and Borough of Leeds, 1425-1662, Thoresby Society, LVII (1983), pp. 6-7). So detailed is the information given about the quantities of building materials used for the repairs, which included the complete rebuilding of the roof, and the kind and duration of the work for which labourers and craftsmen were paid, that Peter was able to work out the dimensions of the building and deduce that the roof was edged with expensive stone roofing slate from Woodhouse quarries. Wooden laths covered the majority of the roof but because these could be easily lifted on a windy day the stone slate was used to weigh down the edges. He based the style of roof on that of the Merchant Adventurers' Hall in York and the oven on one at Gainsborough Old Hall, Lincolnshire; both contemporary buildings. The exact location of the building was established by reference to the sale plan of 'The Shambles Estate' in February 1836 (see Thoresby Society, Plan 36b).

Ralph Thoresby's House
No single contemporary detailed description or drawing of Ralph Thoresby's house exists. Deceived by the watercolour painting of c. 1850 and Hobson's street view of 1878 indicating that they showed Thoresby's house, for many years it has been wrongly believed that his house was simply the brick-fronted two-bayed building depicted in these images. We were not convinced and assembled a great variety of fragmentary pieces of information about the house to try to form a definitive picture of what it was like. This process was greatly assisted by the work of Professor Peter Meredith published in his Thoresby Society Notes from the Library (No. 5, December 2012). The most significant piece of the jigsaw was discovered by Peter Meredith in the Thoresby Society archives in MS Box IV item 33, a small envelope addressed to the Hon Librarian and postmarked Salt Lake City, Utah, 2 December 1941 at 8.00 pm. Inside was a tracing of an original plan of Ralph's Kirkgate property made c. 1724 for Richard Wilson, the eminent lawyer, the friend and executor of Ralph, who had helped to arrange the sale of the estate (see p.46). This tracing, made by someone on 19 November 1889, was accompanied by a very detailed key. This plan was transferred on to the relevant section of the 6 inch to the mile Ordnance Survey plan of Kirkgate in order to draw it to scale. It was thus possible for the first time to identify the original bounds of the plot and the footprints and uses of the structures to the rear of the house.

After much discussion, the penny dropped that 'Thoresby's house' shown on the watercolour and Hobson's drawing was merely the right-hand third of the house's street elevation. What the 1724 plan also revealed, to our great surprise, was that the 1719 Samuel Buck sketch of Thoresby's museum and garden (British Library Lansdowne MS 914), previously assumed to show its southern elevation, actually showed its east facing elevation, and that the area depicted ran across the bottom of his property, rather than facing up it.

With these entirely new insights and information, Peter Brears was able draw his superb bird's eye view of Thoresby's house, museum and outbuildings. Specifically with regard to the museum and garden, it should be noted that Buck intended that his sketch would form the basis for an engraving. A close inspection of it reveals considerable detail of the roof-slates, the voussoirs of the arches, and small sample sections of the brickwork. Items from Thoresby's museum, including the whale rib and scapula, the Scottish targe, stone cannon balls and the niche from St William's Shrine in York (over the upper door) can be seen.

The tower, at the end of the garden, indicated on the 1724 plan, had been built by Mr Bickerdyke, a Norwich merchant; towers of this kind were common in East Anglia, where they were used for business purposes. Peter has used existing examples from that area to inform the design of the tower shown in his picture.

The cross-sections of the house are based on Peter's expert analysis of a number of pieces of evidence: the watercolour painting of c.1850; a Victorian lantern slide showing the 'missing' left-hand two-thirds of the house's street elevation which we very recently discovered in the Thoresby Society Collection; and the series of four accurate sketches made by W. A. Hobson in February 1878, just before the demolition of the property (some of which it is now clear related to the interior of the 'missing' two-thirds of the house). The internal arrangement of the rooms was gleaned from the *'Memorandums respecting Ralph Thoresby and description of his House'*, which accompanied the plan and key. Additional information appeared in an article *'Leeds from Past to Present'* in The Yorkshire Owl (1896); Edmund Bogg's, *Roundabout Leeds* (Leeds, 1902), p. 82; and D.H. Atkinson's, *Ralph Thoresby, the Topographer: His Town and Times* (Leeds, 1887), Vol. 1, pp. 61-62. The house with its observatory appears indistinctly on Samuel Buck's *East Prospect of the Town of Leedes* made in October 1719 from Cavalier Hill. Ralph makes occasional reference to his house and museum in the *'Review of His Life 1658-1714'*; the original is in the Yorkshire Archaeological Society's collections MS 26 and a transcription with an introduction by Professor Peter Meredith appears in The Thoresby Society's *Ducatus Tercentenary Volume II* (Leeds, 2015). Ralph's diaries, edited by J. Hunter (1830) also contain some additional information.

Finally, having discovered the lantern slide of the 'missing' two-thirds of the street elevation, we could not resist challenging our excellent book designer, Paul Dean, to use his skills to merge this late-Victorian image with the watercolour of c. 1850 to create an overall impression of the front elevation of Thoresby's house. It must be remembered that Thoresby had the jetties of his timber-framed house sawn off and its front clad in brick in 1708, and it was much altered by the time Fourness the chemists had taken it over in the late Victorian period; nevertheless it is a thrill for us to reveal the frontage of our hero's house for the first time in over 130 years, just as it was for us to see Peter Brears' splendid bird's eye view of it.

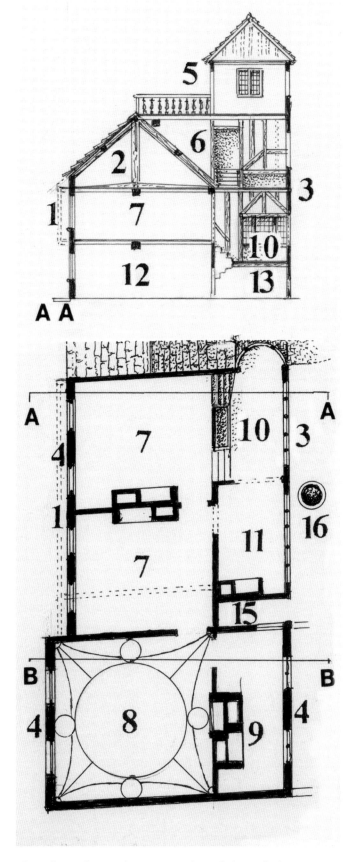

First Floor Plan and Cross-section of Thoresby's House. (PB) Kirkgate is on the left.
Key: *1. Former jetty; 2. 16th-century half-timbered gables; 3. 17th-century half-timbered north gables; 4. 1708 brick façade; 5. Observatory; 6. Stairs to observatory; 7. Chambers; 8. Drawing Room; 9. Chimney of 1678; 10. Study; 11. Library (over Dining Room); 12. 'Good sized room'; 13. Entrance Hall and stairs; 14. Shop? (not shown but under 8); 15. North end of entry passage from Kirkgate; 16. Draw-well in yard.*

The Residents of Leeds Kirkgate in 1692

Assessment to maintain the war against France

An Assessment made this 5th July 1692 By vertue of a Warrant to us directed by the Commissioners appointed by a certain Act of Parliament entitled [An Act for raising Moneys by a Poll payable Quarterly, for one yeare for carrying on a Vigourous Warr against France] raised taxed & assessed for Leeds Kirkgate.

	£	s.	d.
Charles Clarkson junr & wife		2	0
Wm Kent, Tradesman, wife & Labourer		13	0
Mr. John Spink, Attorney, wife, child & maid	1	4	0
Mr. Smeaton		1	0
Wm Atkinson, Samuel Atkinson, wife, 2 children, 1 man & 1 maid		7	0
Benjamin Harrison		1	0
Ralph Thoresby, wife, child & maid		14	0
Dr Jaques, wife & maid		3	0
Christopher Conder, wife, 2 children & 1 maid		15	0
Mr. Samuel Ibbetson, Marcht, wife, 3 children, 2 maids	1	7	0
Mrs. Elizah Ibbetson, daughter & maid		3	0
Mr. ...las Dunwel, Trademan, wife, 2 children, 1 maid, 1 App.		16	0
Mrs. Dunwel senr 1s, Mr Dixon 1s		2	0
Mr. Killingbeck, Vicar, wife & 2 maids	1	4	0
Edward Brooksbank		1	0
James Conjers & wife		2	0
Lambert Bilton, Tradesman, wife, 2 children, 1 maid, 1 app.		16	0
Timothy Fearnsides & wife		2	0
Robert Conjers & daughter		2	0
Robert Hague, wife, 2 children & 1 maid		5	0
Wm. Burrow, wife & child		3	0
Edmd Dodshon, Trademan, wife, 2 children & 1 maid		15	0
Joseph Conder, wife, 4 children & 1 maid		7	0
John Procter & wife		2	0
Robert Tetlaw & wife		2	0
Richard Gowland		1	0
Bryan Procter & wife		2	0
Wm Haxby & wife		2	0
John Layton		1	0
John Nicolson & wife		2	0
Mr. Robt Pickersgil, Tradesman, wife, son & maid		13	0
John Waid, wife and daughter		3	0
Widdow Tessimond		1	0
Francis Mawd, wife & child		3	0
John Bretherlck		1	0
Thomas Pease, wife & 2 children		4	0
Mr. Wm Cookson, Tradesman, wife, 4 children, 2 maids, 1 appr.		19	0
Thomas Marshall		1	0
Wm Marshall, wife & child		3	0
Mr. Christopher Pawson, wife, son & maid		14	0
Mr. Henry Pawson, Marcht, wife & maid	1	3	0
Mr. Bright Dixon, wife, 4 children, 2 maids		8	0
Robert Hudson, wife & mother		3	0
Joseph Pullen, wife & child		3	0
Mr. Rd Dickons, Attornay, child & maid [crossed out 'removed']		0	0
Thomas Johnson, Apprentice & maid		3	0
Edmund Stephenson [crossed out 'removed']		0	0
Henry French		1	0

James Cocker		1	0
Mrs. Overing		1	0
Widdow Clifton 1s, Mr Benson 1s		2	0
Widdow Blackburn		1	0
Thomas Harrison & wife		2	0
Mrs. Smithson & 2 children		3	0
Daniel Noble		1	0
Saml Andrew		1	0
John Pease, wife, 3 children & Mrs Milner		6	0
Widdow Harrison		1	0
Robt Forge, wife, 1 child, 2 servants		5	0
John Harrison, wife & daughter		3	0
John Lindley, wife & 1 child & maid		4	0
Matthew Wilkinson, Tradesman, wife, child		13	0
Mr. Samuel Barlow, wife & maid		3	0
Christopher Harrison, wife, 4 children		6	0
Wm Prest & wife		2	0
Robt Hill, wife, maid & Apprentice		4	0
Francis Mitchel		1	0
John Simson		1	0
Edwd Bolton & wife		2	0
Widdow Bolton		1	0
Thomas Parin & wife		2	0
Mr. Wm Cotton, Tradesman, 4 children 2 maids 2 appren'		19	0
Alderman Josha Ibbetson, Commissioner	1	1	0
Mrs. Ibbetson, 3 children, 2 maids & 1 man servt		7	0
Isaac Noble & wife		2	0
John Ellis & wife		2	0
Thomas Watson & son		2	0
Widdow Dixon & 2 daughters		3	0
Mathew Wroes, widow & servant		2	0
Joseph Wroe, wife, 2 children & maid		5	0
Saml Wawbron & wife & child		3	0
Robt Watson, wife & child		3	0
Tho. Hudson, wife child & Apprentice		4	0
Widdow Raper		1	0
John Wroe, wife & child		3	0
John Watson		1	0
Widdow Chipping, 4 children, 1 maid, 1 Apprentice		7	0
Mr. Wm Dodshon, Tradesman, wife, child, 2 maids 4 apprentices		19	0
John Hardwick		1	0
Josa Dawson, wife, & 2 children		4	0
Edmd Greaves, 2 children & 1 Apprentice		4	0
Mr. John Dodshon, Tradesman, 4 children, 1 maid, 1 Apprentice		18	0
James Tennant		1	0
Bryan Brown & maid		2	0
Robt Rayner & wife		2	0
Geo. Watson wife & son		3	0
Seth Shipley		1	0
Mrs. Hannah Brearley & maid		2	0

Asse'd   Sa: Ibbetson   Confirmed by us   John Preston Major
               Ralph Thoresby   Thomas Dixon
Collect^{rs}   Christopr Conder   Wm Massie
               Saml Atkinson

You are hereby Required to Collect the sume above menconed and to pay the same to the Head Collectr at the House of Mrs. Johnson in Leeds the 30th of this Instant June 1692.

Endnotes

1. A. McGuire and A. Clark, *The Leeds Crosses* (Leeds, 1987).

2. C. B. Fawcett, The Location of Leeds, British Association Leeds Meeting General Handbook (Leeds, 1927), pp. 6-19.

3. Venerable Bede, *Historia Ecclesiastica*, (London, 1896), pp.115-116 and C. Corning, *The Baptism of Edwin, King of Northumbria: A New Analysis of the British Tradition*, Northern History, XXXVI (Leeds, 2000) pp. 5-13.

4. S. Burt and K. Grady, *The Illustrated History of Leeds* (Derby, 1994), pp.10-12.

5. H. Hamerow, *Rural Settlement and Society in Anglo-Saxon England,* (Oxford, 2012), pp.46-8.

6. A. Mason, *Religion in Leeds* (Stroud, 1994) and A. McGuire and A. Clark, *The Leeds Crosses* (Leeds, 1987).

7. J. Le Patourel, *The Norman Conquest of Yorkshire*, Northern History, VI, (Leeds, 1971) pp. 1-21 and W. E. Kapelle, *The Norman Conquest of the North* (London, 1979).

8. S. Moorhouse and M. Faull, West Yorkshire: *An archaeological survey to 1500 A.D.*, Volume 4, Map 17 Entries from Domesday Book (Wakefield, 1981).

9. It seems likely that these were all members of the same family and that the Scandinavian preference for partible inheritance meant that a Viking lord had divided his 'estate of Leeds' between his sons.

10. J. Morris (ed.), *Domesday Book* (Chichester, 1996) and H. C. and I. S. Maxwell, *The Domesday Geography of Northern England* (Cambridge, 1962).

11. W. E. Wightman, 'The Yorkshire Lacys, 1066-1193', *University of Leeds Review*, X (Leeds, 1966).

12. By 1379 out of total receipts of £189 16s 0d, Leeds contributed £98 2s 0d, with Holbeck Manor providing a further £5 6s 8d. Ibid. p. 223.

13. Rev. J. Solloway, *The Alien Benedictines of York* (Leeds, 1910).

14. Today this road is 'The Calls'. *The English Dialect Dictionary* (Oxford, 1923) tells us that CAAL written 'Call' was an old West Yorkshire dialect word referring to a mill dam or weir, or the outlet or channel of water flowing from a dam. In the Middle Ages the huge 'High Dam' (now under Leeds railway station) and 'Bondman Dam' near Swinegate diverted channels of water from the River Aire to power the manorial corn mill (now under Criterion Place car park) and the fulling mills on either side of Leeds Bridge. The channel of water or mill race flowed across the back of Warehouse Hill, parallel with The Calls, and back into the river at the east end of Warehouse Hill close to today's Centenary Footbridge. Almost certainly The Calls took its name from this complex of weirs and goits. Thoresby (*Ducatus* p. 76) was clearly unaware of the Yorkshire origin of the word 'Call' and speculated that The Calls took its name from the Latin 'Callis' meaning a beaten path.

15. D. Hey, *The Oxford Companion to Local and Family History*, (Oxford, 1996), pp. 440-1.

16. Elements of a planned layout for the village are evident on the southern side of Kirkgate just below the junction with Call Lane. A double-width plot, measuring 58 feet is today occupied by the First White Cloth Hall.

17. C. T. Clay (ed.), Early Yorkshire Charters, Vol. VI, *The Paynell Fee,* YAS Record Series Extra Series, III (1939), pp. 68-9.

18. M. W. Beresford and H. P. R. Finberg, *English Medieval Boroughs: A Handlist* (Newton Abbot, 1973), pp. 21-61. In the period 1201-1250, 135 new boroughs were created in England but only four in Yorkshire.

19. J. Le Patourel, *Manor and Borough of Leeds*, Thoresby Society, XLV (1956), p. 9.

20. It is not known where these were originally sited but it is possible that the oven was located in the 'island' shown on Cossins' Plan of 1726 at Kirkgate End, later the site of the new prison.

21. J. Kirkby, *The Manor and Borough of Leeds,* 1425-1662: *An edition of Documents,* Thoresby Society, LVII, (1983), pp.6-7.

22. *Ibid*., p. 13.

23. *Ibid*., p. 47.

24. J. Rusby, *St Peter's at Leeds: being an account historical and descriptive of The Parish Church* (Leeds, 1896), pp. 21-2.

25. G. C. F. Forster, 'The foundations: from the earliest times to c.1700' in *A Modern History of Leeds* (ed. D. Fraser (Manchester, 1980), p. 7.

26. Calendar Patent Rolls, 8 Edw II, M20D, p. 236.

27. E. K. Clark, 'A Brawl in Kirkgate', *Thoresby Society*, IV (1895), pp. 125-138.

28. Le Patourel, 'Manor and Borough of Leeds', pp. 56-66.

29. *Ibid.*, p.70.

30. R. Thoresby, *Vicaria Leodiensis* (1724), pp.20-1; Thoresby Society, XLV (1956), pp. 50-55.

31. R. V. Taylor, *Biographia Leodiensis or Worthies of Leeds* (Leeds, 1865), pp. 72-3.

32. R. Thoresby, *Ducatus Leodiensis* (1715), p. 37.

33. *Yorkshire Chantry Surveys, Volume II*, The Surtees Society Volume 92 (Durham, 1893) p. 216.

34. Thoresby, *Ducatus*, p. 38.

35. D. Whomsley, 'William Ramsden of Longley, Gentleman 1514-1580, Agent in Monastic Property', *Yorkshire Archaeological Journal* 42 (2) (Leeds,1968), pp. 43-150.

36. The authors are extremely grateful to J. M. Collinson and J. L. Cruickshank for sharing their research. See TNA E 318/ Box18/920 (37 Henry VIII: 1545), YAS DD 10 I 31, the transcript of which is in Leeds District Archives WYL 500/ 925. Summary in Letters and Papers Henry VIII 20 pt.1 p.526. The deed of partition is in Leeds District Archives WYL 179/438/.

37. York Corporation Minute Books, xxiii, f.20a, 8 June 1561.

38. H. Heaton, *The Yorkshire Woollen and Worsted Industries: From the Earliest Times up to the Industrial Revolution* (Oxford, 1965), pp. 56-7.

39. Revd C. B. Norcliffe, 'Local Muniments – Documents concerning…the Pawson property in Kirkgate and Knowstrop, Leeds', *Yorkshire Archaeological Journal, III* (1875), pp. 64-80.

40. Revd C. B. Norcliffe, 'The Pawson Inventory and Pedigree', Thoresby Society, Miscellany, IV (1895), pp. 164-68.

41. This section on the production of woollen cloth was kindly written by Peter Brears.

42. Thoresby, *Vicaria Leodiensis*, pp. 6, 28-9 and 36-7.

43. A. C. Price, *A History of Leeds Grammar School* (Leeds, 1919), p. 59.

44. J. G. Davies, *From Bridge to Moor: The History of Leeds Grammar School from its foundation to 1854* (Leeds, 2002), pp. 1-8. Provision in the town may date from as early as the fourteenth century.

45. West Yorkshire Archive Service (Leeds), DB213/47, Littlewood Petition, 1598.

46. Thoresby Society Manuscript Box 1 (18) Transcript of Commission appointed by Queen Elizabeth 1 to take evidence in a suit between the tenants of Leeds Kirkgate and John Lyndley and others, defendants 42 Elizabeth (1599) and property in Leeds held by the Duchy of Lancaster. Exchequer Special Commissions 2803 (York).

47. E 178/ 2801 Special Commission.

48. The jury declared that following were tenants of the manor and dwelt in it, namely:
Christopher Hodgeson, Thomas Cowper, Thomas Lickborrowe, Widow Atwell, Dyonise Stockdale, William Clark, John Gibson, Widow Browne, Richard Sykes, Elizabeth Fether, Henry Adcock, William Grave, Alexander Fletcher, Bryan Iles, Nicholas Partriche, John Martin, John Sykes, Marie Lightfoote, Henrie Heldricke, Christopher Pawson, Mathew Cowper, Richard Wade, Charles Sawle, Widow Wilkinson, James Holgate, Rainold Wilson, Michael Hargrave, the land of Mr. Smith, Robert Boothe and Bryan Boothe, William Marshall, Widow Watson, Abraham Hargrave, John Mawson, Berichus Ambler, Thomas Cromocke, Christopher Boyes, William Swallow, Peter West, William Brodeley, Robert Ardron, John Foxe, William Altofts, Martin Beckwith, Robert Dixon, George Watson, Thomas Cromock, Henry Curtesse, Ralph Iles, The Vicaredge, George Greene, Gregorie Langscarrey, Hughe Morgan, Thomas Gibson, Robert Kidd, William Thomlinson, Christopher Seele with certaine cottage under Cald bancke dwelling in Leedes Kirkgate (being sometime parcel of the Trinities late dissolved do hold their dwellinghouses of the Crowne and not of the Duchie).

49. J. Kirkby, *The Manor and Borough of Leeds, 1425-1662: An edition of Documents*, Thoresby Society, LVII, (1983), pp. 245-9.

50. A. F. Upton, *Sir Arthur Ingram, 1565-1642, A Study in the Origins of an English Landed Gentry* (1961), p. 45.

51. *Ibid.*, pp. 155-6.

52. J. Kirkby, 'The Manor and Borough of Leeds: 1425-1662: An Edition of Documents', Thoresby Society, LVII (1983), pp. 155-205.

53. J. W. Kirkby, 'A Leeds Elite: the Principal Burgesses of the First Leeds Corporation', *Northern History, XX (1984), p. 106.*

54. Their third child, William Lowther II, was born in the house in 1639. The family quickly outgrew this accommodation and by November 1642 had moved to larger premises on Briggate, which became a haven for Royalist sympathisers. In 1688 William II (1639-1705) inherited his father's estate and moved to Great Preston Hall. He became a great benefactor to Ralph Thoresby, giving many items, including autographs of the famous, to his museum.

55. J. Kirkby, 'The Aldermen of Leeds 1626-1700', Thoresby Society, LXIV (2008), pp. 80-82.

56. West Yorkshire Archives Service, Leeds, WYL100/M14/4. The authors are grateful to Michael and Catherine Collinson for their generosity in sharing this information with them.

57. Will and inventory of William Dixon, dated 8 March 1663 (Borthwick Institute of Historical Research, University of York).

58. J. Wardell, *The Municipal History of the Borough of Leeds in the County of York from the earliest period to the 1st January 1836 (Leeds, 1846), pp. xci-xciii.*

59. J. Kirkby, 'Aldermen of Leeds 1626-1700', pp. 69-70.

60. R. G. Wilson, 'Merchants and Land: The Ibbetsons of Leeds and Denton, 1650-1850', Northern History, XIV (1988), pp. 75-83.

61. The authors are grateful to John Goodchild for allowing the use of his extensive research in the writing of this section of the book; see John Goodchild Collection Research File 83F. For the Cookson pedigree, see Revd T. D. Whitaker, *Ducatus Leodiensis*, 2nd edition (Leeds, 1816), p. 136.

62. Leeds Parish Registers, *Thoresby Society*, X (Leeds, 1898), p. 17.

63. G. D. Lumb (ed.), MSS. Written or Possessed by Ralph Thoresby, F.R.S., *Thoresby Society*, XXVIII, (Leeds, 1927), pp.444-7.

64. Court Book of Leeds Corporation (First Book), *Thoresby Society, XXXIV* (Leeds, 1933), p. 8, 30 September 1682.

65. *Ibid.*, p. 10.

66. *Ibid.*, p. 30.

67. *Ibid.,* p. 31.

68. *Ibid.*, p. 93.

69. Burt and Grady, The *Illustrated History of Leeds*, p. 34.

70. West Yorkshire Archive Service (Wakefield), 1709, B, 24, 11.

71. Wilson, 'Merchants and Land', pp. 74-100.

72. Heaton, *The Yorkshire Woollen and Worsted Industries*, pp. 323-58.

73. Daniel Defoe, *A Tour Through the Whole Island of Great Britain (1724-6)*, (Penguin edition ed. P. Rogers, 1971), pp. 500-5.

74. *Ibid.*, p. 364.

75. Revd J. Hunter, ed., *The Diaries of Ralph Thoresby F.R.S.* (1830).

76. R.Thoresby, *Ducatus Leodiensis,* p. 249-250.

77. Hunter, *Diary of Ralph Thoresby,* vol. 2, p. 77.

78. The first assembly was held in the cloth hall on 11 June 1712 see also *Leeds Mercury,* 20 September 1726.

79. *Leeds Mercury,* 24 July 1739.

80. *Leeds Mercury*, 11 December 1759 and *Leeds Intelligencer,* 11 December 1765.

81. J. Singleton, 'Extract from an Old Leeds Merchant's Memorandum Book, 1777', *Thoresby Society,* XXIV (1919), p. 35.

82. *Leeds Intelligencer,* 13 and 20 January 1789.

83. *Leeds Mercury,* 13 October 1778.

84. M. W. Beresford, 'Observations on East Prospect of Leedes in Yorkshire from Chaveler Hill', *Thoresby Society,* LXIV (2008), pp. 127-131.

85. J. Ryley, *The Leeds Guide* (1806), p. 65.

86. *Leeds Intelligencer,* 10 October 1780 and *Leeds Mercury,* 3 October 1780. James Ibbetson invested heavily in redeveloping the site and when his grandson, Sir James Ibbetson (1746-95) came to sell the property in 1771 it comprised houses, workshops, a brew house and stable with chambers and granaries over the top. In addition there were Sir James' own stables, coach house and

chaise house, along with privies, a large dung hill and a sizeable piece of vacant ground (West Yorkshire Archive Service (Wakefield), 1771, BM, 670,848). Some of these dwelling houses were of a decent standard as former tenants included a clergyman and a wealthy widow (*Leeds Mercury*, 16 Jan 1770). Sir James was busy rebuilding Denton Hall and lacked the capital and inclination to further develop the site (*Leeds Intelligencer*, 26 Feb.1771). This opportunity was seized upon by others. Two of the purchasers, Jeremiah Dixon of Gledhow Hall and Thomas Lee of Briggate, were successful merchants. They were joined in the venture by John Caygill of Halifax and James Hanson, a yeoman farmer of Colton. Over the next fifteen years more houses, shops, workshops and warehouses were erected on the vacant ground. Thus by the end of the eighteenth century this was an intensely developed plot and over-crowding was clearly becoming an issue. With limited access to water and primitive sanitary arrangements this became a less desirable location in which to work and reside. Hunter, *Diary of Ralph Thoresby*, pp. 315 and 323.

[87.] P. Meredith (ed.), *Ralph Thoresby's Review of His Life 1658-1714* [Yorkshire Archaeological Society MS26], The Thoresby Society's Ducatus Tercentenary Publication, Vol. 2 (Leeds,2015), p. 187.

[88.] Burt and Grady, The *Illustrated History of Leeds*, p. 32.

[89.] P. C. D. Brears, 'Ralph Thoresby, A Museum Visitor in Stuart England', The Thoresby Society's Ducatus Tercentenary Publication, vol. 1, pp. 93-115.

[90.] Hunter, *The Diary of Ralph Thoresby*, vol. 1, p. 14.

[91.] E. A. Kent, *The Mayors of Norwich 1403-1835*, (Norwich, 1938). He was councillor 1676-82, alderman 1683-7and 1688-1701 and mayor in 1696. He had been born in Farnham, Yorkshire and his family had connections to Leeds.

[92.] Thoresby Society, MS Box SD 9 (w).

[93.] E. Harley, Historical Manuscripts Commission VI (Portland MSS).

[94.] *Leeds Mercury*, 7 September 1725.

[95.] *Leeds Mercury*, 12 October 1725.

[96.] P. Meredith, *Ralph* 'Thoresby's House in Kirkgate, Leeds', Thoresby Society, Notes from the Library (No. 5, December 2012) and H. Murray, *Scarborough, York and Leeds: the Town Plans of John Cossins 1697-1743* (York, 1997), pp. 63-91.

[97.] D. H. Atkinson, *Ralph Thoresby, the Topographer, his town and times, vol.2* (Leeds, 1887), p. 434. The Leeds Library holds a wonderful copy of *Ducatus Leodiensis* with annotations in the hand of Thomas Wilson, wherein he describes in the margin the fate of various items of the collection.

[98.] R. G. Wilson, 'Merchants and Land', pp. 76-85.

[99.] The tithe barn remained for almost another hundred years until its demolition for the erection of the Leeds National School in 1812.

[100.] Thoresby, *Ducatus*, p. 249.

[101.] H. Murray, *The Town Plans of John Cossins*, p. 83.

[102.] *Leeds Mercury*, 22 August 1738.

[103.] T. F. Friedman, '*James Parmentier in Leeds: A Newly Discovered Drawing*', Leeds Arts Calendar, No 94 (Leeds, 1984).

[104.] J. Oates, '*Leeds and the Jacobite Rebellions*', Thoresby Society (2004), pp. 4-5.

[105.] Leeds Local and Family History Library, *Diary of John Lucas*, p. 51.

[106.] Thoresby, *Ducatus*, p.107.

[107.] *Leeds Mercury,* 23 November 1725.

[108.] R. G. Wilson, 'Ossington and the Denisons', *History Today*, XVIII (1968), pp.168-172.

[109.] *Leeds Intelligencer,* 29 July 1777.

[110.] A. Kidson, *George Romney 1734-1802* (2002), pp. 22-4.

[111.] *Leeds Intelligencer,* 16 April 1782; *Leeds Mercury*, 30 April 1782 and R. Jackson, *New Illustrated Guide to Leeds and Environs* (Leeds, 1889), p. 191.

[112.] *Leeds Intelligencer,* 15 June 1762.

[113.] F. Beckwith, *The Leeds Library 1768-1968* (Leeds, 1968), pp. 1-6.

[114.] M. W. Beresford, *East End, West End: The face of Leeds during urbanisation 1684-1842,* Thoresby Society, LX and LXI (Leeds,1985-6), p. 76.

[115.] *Ibid.*, p. 105.

[116.] M. W. Beresford, 'The Face of Leeds 1780-1914', in Fraser, History of *Modern Leeds*, pp.75-6. By 1839 notoriously there were 36 cottages crammed into the yard.

[117.] W. G. Rimmer, 'Working Men's Cottages in Leeds 1770-1840', *Thoresby Society,* Miscellany XIII, Part 2, (1961), f.n. p. 170.

[118.] *Leeds Intelligencer,* 11 August 1767.

[119.] *Leeds Mercury,* 30 January 1781.

[120.] John Goodchild Research File 83F.

[121.] Leeds Local and Family History Library, *Extracts from the Summersgill Collection*, vol. 3, p. 117.

[122.] *Leeds Mercury,* 29 July 1777. These houses are still standing today.

[123.] *Leeds Mercury,* 6 Feb 1776.

[124.] *Leeds Intelligencer*, 16 March 1773.

[125.] *The Leeds Guide* (1806), p. 75.

Acknowledgments

First and foremost we gratefully acknowledge the work of Peter Brears whose superb illustrations have added so much to our understanding of many of the most important buildings on Kirkgate. The quality look and feel of this publication is down to the skill of Paul Dean of Leeds City Council's Creative Services Team. We greatly appreciate the support of the University of Huddersfield and, in particular, the research undertaken by Thomas Allen and Mark McCabe on the site of the Golden Cock Inn and the Manor House. Special mention must be made of the following people who so generously shared their research with us or commented on the interpretation of the evidence—Catherine and Michael Collinson, John Cruickshank, John Goodchild, Peter Meredith, Ian Sanderson and Stuart Wrathmell. Our thanks too to Eveleigh Bradford and John Townsend of the Thoresby Society, staff at the West Yorkshire Archive Service, Leeds Museums and Galleries, Leeds City Council's Legal Department and the Leeds Local and Family History Library, who cheerfully brought us literally thousands of documents, photographs, books, maps and newspapers for our perusal. Special thanks to Don Cole and Peter and Greta Meredith who kindly gave constructive feedback on the draft of the book and to Cath Follin and Kerry Harker who painstakingly checked the final copy for errors. We have greatly benefited from the support of Phil Ward and Neall Bower of Leeds City Council's Sustainable Development Unit who have given constant encouragement to us. Finally we would like to thank the Heritage Lottery Fund, Leeds City Council and Leeds Civic Trust whose generous financial support made possible the publication of this work through the Lower Kirkgate Townscape Heritage Initiative.

Steven Burt and Kevin Grady
March 2016

About the authors

Steven Burt is Visiting Professor of History at the University of Huddersfield, Vice-President of the Thoresby Society, a trustee of Thackray Medical Research Trust and the Paul Thackray Heritage Foundation. He is former Museum Director of the Royal Armouries and Area Manager for Education Leeds. He was born and bred in Leeds and has been communicating his enthusiasm for history and heritage to the widest possible audience through lecturing, teaching, research, writing and broadcasting. His lifelong interest in the history of Leeds was recognised in 2008 when he became a finalist in Leeds Civic Trust's Spirit of Leeds Award. In 2010 his contribution to education was formally acknowledged when he received an Honorary Doctorate of Education from Leeds Metropolitan University. He and Kevin Grady wrote the now classic work on the history of the city, *The Illustrated History of Leeds*, first published in 1994.

Kevin Grady has been Director of Leeds Civic Trust since 1987. He graduated from Leeds University in economic history in 1972, and then completed a PhD, since published as a Thoresby Society monograph, on the Georgian Public Buildings of Leeds and the West Riding of Yorkshire. He was a lecturer in Economic History at Leeds Metropolitan University, Exeter University and Leeds University before taking up his present post. He has published extensively on the history of Leeds and is particularly well known for his tremendously popular annual series of lunch time lectures on the history of Leeds given at Holy Trinity Church, Boar Lane, over the last decade. In 2014 he was awarded an Honorary Doctorate of Arts by Leeds Metropolitan University in recognition of his services to the City of Leeds.

Peter Brears, FSA, Peter Brears graduated from Leeds College of Art in 1968, then worked in various museums, mostly directing the city museums of York and then Leeds, where he opened the Armley Mills, Thwaite Mills and Georgian museums, establishing the Leeds Waterfront Heritage Trail and initiated the conservation of Kirkstall Abbey. His removal from Leeds Museums in 1994 enabled him to fulfil the increasing demands on his research and development skills from Historic Royal Palaces, English Heritage, Cadw, the National Trust, major stately homes and museum trusts. His numerous books and academic articles on castles, museums, post-medieval archaeology, country pottery, folk art and food history are accepted as standard works in their respective fields. His books and booklets on Leeds include *Images of Leeds, A Taste of Leeds* and *A Leeds Life.*

Lower Kirkgate Townscape Heritage Initiative

The Lower Kirkgate Townscape Heritage Initiative was established in 2012 with funds from the Heritage Lottery Fund. One of the primary aims of the initiative is to reverse the physical and economic decline of this historic area in order to make lower Kirkgate a place people want to visit once more, both for business and pleasure. To do so it seeks to address the evident market failure by bringing the vacant and underused buildings back into use.

In acknowledging the historic importance of the area the scheme funds 'conservation standard' works. This means that repair is favoured rather than replacement and, where appropriate, reinstatement using traditional designs and methods reflecting the traditional construction of the buildings and their architectural form. Once the work is complete the buildings are able to be used again and contribute to the economy of the city both in terms of increased trade and jobs, hence the term 'heritage led regeneration'.

An added benefit of this approach is that it not only brings about the required aesthetic improvement and economic benefits but also supports key traditional heritage skills which are currently in decline such as joinery and metal work amongst others, and gives the opportunity for trainees to learn new skills.

However, the initiative is not only about creating attractive, vibrant places that people want to work, visit and invest in. It is also about inspiring communities to find out more about their townscape heritage. This publication plays an important role in telling us much about the area that we did not know and additional detail about subjects already familiar to us.

This will encourage people to find out more about an important part of the city to which they may not have given a great deal of thought. This book has been funded by the Lower Kirkgate Townscape Heritage Initiative with this aim and in the hope that what is understood is valued, sustained and protected.

Leeds Civic Trust

Founded in 1965, Leeds Civic Trust is an independent, non-political, voluntary organisation made up of people who live and work in Leeds and are keen to promote its improvement. Its principal aims are to encourage:

- High standards of architecture and planning
- Conservation and enhancement of the city's heritage
- Improvements of public amenities and the quality of life.

Having our offices, local history bookshop and exhibition room in a pair of Victorian cottages in The Calls, we have had a long-standing interest in the regeneration of Kirkgate. For a curious combination of circumstances, the remarkable regeneration of many parts of Leeds city centre over the last three decades has been slow to reach the heart of the original settlement. We have therefore embraced and supported the Lower Kirkgate Townscape Heritage Initiative with great enthusiasm. The writing of this book by the Trust's Director, Dr Kevin Grady, and his long-time co-author and member of the Trust, Professor Steven Burt, is part of our contribution to demonstrating why Kirkgate and the First White Cloth Hall are of such great significance in the history of Leeds.

Leeds Civic Trust, 19 Wharf Street, Leeds, LS2 7EQ
Telephone: 0113 243 9594; e-mail: office@leedscivictrust.org.uk;
Website: www.leedscivictrust.org.uk; Registered Charity No. 10104362